PATHWAYS

Reading, Writing, and Critical Thinking

1

Mari Vargo
Laurie Blass
Nancy Hubley

NATIONAL GEOGRAPHIC LEARNING | HEINLE CENGAGE Learning

Australia • Brazil • Japan • Korea • Mexico • Singapore • Spain • United Kingdom • United States

Pathways 1 Teacher's Guide

Publisher: Andrew Robinson

Executive Editor: Sean Bermingham

Senior Development Editor: Bill Preston

Development Editor: Karen Davy

Director of Global Marketing: Ian Martin

Marketing Manager: Emily Stewart

Director of Content and Media Production: Michael Burggren

Sr. Content Project Manager: Daisy Sosa

Manufacturing Buyer: Marybeth Hennebury

Cover Design: Page 2 LLC

Cover Image: Julien Gille/iStockphoto

Interior Design: Page 2 LLC, Cenveo Publisher Services/Nesbitt Graphics, Inc.

Composition: Cenveo® Publisher Services

ISBN-13: 978-1-133-31734-0

ISBN-10: 1-133-31734-0

National Geographic Learning
20 Channel Center St.
Boston, MA 02210
USA

Cengage Learning is a leading provider of customized learning solutions with office locations around the globe, including Singapore, the United Kingdom, Australia, Mexico, Brazil, and Japan. Locate your local office at: **international.cengage.com/region**

Cengage Learning products are represented in Canada by Nelson Education, Ltd.

Visit National Geographic Learning online at **ngl.cengage.com**
Visit our corporate website at **www.cengage.com**

Printed in the United States of America
1 2 3 4 5 6 7 8 15 14 13

TABLE OF CONTENTS

Advantages of *Pathways Reading, Writing, and Critical Thinking*

In *Pathways Reading, Writing, and Critical Thinking*, real-world content from *National Geographic* publications provides a context for meaningful language acquisition. Students learn essential, high-frequency vocabulary, review important grammatical structures, and practice reading and writing skills that will allow them to succeed in academic settings.

Pathways Reading, Writing, and Critical Thinking can be used in a wide variety of language-learning programs, from high schools and community colleges to private language institutes and intensive English programs. The high-interest content motivates students and teachers alike.

The following features are included in *Pathways Reading, Writing, and Critical Thinking*:

- Academic Pathways goals at the beginning of each unit give students and teachers clear performance objectives.

- Opening pages introduce the unit theme and provide key vocabulary and concepts.

- Readings in a variety of academic content areas and genres present target vocabulary and provide ideas for writing.

- An audio program includes recordings of all the reading texts.

- Clear grammar charts present key structures and language for writing assignments.

- An *Independent Student Handbook* and Vocabulary Index serve as tools to use in class or for self-study and review.

Teaching Language Skills and Academic Literacy

Students need more than language skills to succeed in an academic setting. In addition to teaching the English language, the *Pathways* series teaches academic literacy, which includes not only reading, writing, speaking, and listening skills, but also visual literacy, classroom participation and collaboration skills, critical thinking, and the ability to use technology for learning. Students today are expected to be motivated, inquisitive, original, and creative. In short, they're expected to possess quite an extensive skills set before they even begin their major course of study.

Using *National Geographic* Content in a Language Class

The use of high-interest content from real *National Geographic* publications sets the *Pathways* series apart. Students are engaged by fascinating stories about real people and places around the world and the important issues that affect us all.

High-interest reading passages provide opportunities to practice reading and critical thinking skills, while providing vocabulary and ideas for writing assignments.

The topics in *Pathways Reading, Writing, and Critical Thinking* correspond to academic subject areas and appeal to a wide range of interests. For example:

Academic Subject Area	Unit Title	Unit Theme
Sociology/Education	*Learning Experiences*	an 84-year-old man goes to school, an African gray parrot shows cognitive skills, and a program in Los Angeles uses nature to inspire inner-city learners
History/Anthropology	*Family Ties*	a research project uses DNA to trace the history of human migration, and studies of DNA and ancient human remains show how all humans today share a common ancestry
Environmental Science/ Sociology	*The Trouble with Trash*	an "island" of plastic grows in the Pacific Ocean, a sculptor makes human sculptures with trash, and an artist creates images of workers at a huge landfill in Brazil
Art/Music	*Musicians with a Message*	an extraordinary band encourages people to "look beyond appearances" and to be positive and strong, and three musicians use music to make a difference
Life Science/Anthropology	*Behavior*	an animal trainer helps dogs and dog owners deal with their problems, gorillas in the wild show an ability to use tools, and a study shows that capuchin monkeys, like humans, expect fair treatment

Increasing Visual Literacy

Photographs, maps, charts, and graphs can all convey enormous amounts of information. Lecturers and professors rarely present information without some kind of visual aid. Helping students to make sense of visuals is an important part of preparing them for academic success.

Ocean Impact

Human activities are affecting, in some way, all of the world's oceans. These activities include fishing, farming, manufacturing, and offshore gas and oil drilling.

Maps are used in the *Pathways* series not only to show locations and geographical features, but also to illustrate historical facts and current trends—both local and global. In an academic setting, the ability to read maps is expected, and *Pathways* gives students opportunities to hone that skill.

Impact of human activity

- ■ Very high
- ■ High
- ■ Medium high
- ■ Medium
- ■ Low
- ■ Very low

Charts and graphs present numerical data in a visual way, and the *Pathways* series gives students practice in reading them.

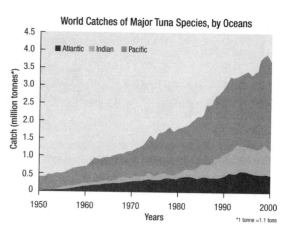

World Catches of Major Tuna Species, by Oceans

Pathways uses a variety of graphic organizers to present content. Graphic organizers appeal to visual learners by showing relationships between ideas in a visual way. Students use graphic organizers for a number of reading and writing tasks such as note taking, comparing similarities and differences, brainstorming, identifying main ideas and details, and organizing notes for writing assignments.

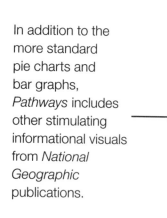

In addition to the more standard pie charts and bar graphs, *Pathways* includes other stimulating informational visuals from *National Geographic* publications.

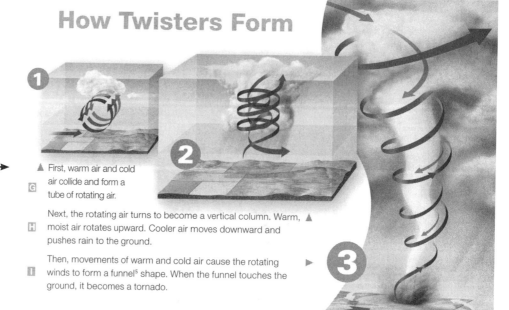

How Twisters Form

▲ First, warm air and cold air collide and form a tube of rotating air.

Next, the rotating air turns to become a vertical column. Warm, ▲ moist air rotates upward. Cooler air moves downward and pushes rain to the ground.

Then, movements of warm and cold air cause the rotating ► winds to form a funnel⁵ shape. When the funnel touches the ground, it becomes a tornado.

Building Critical Thinking Skills

Critical thinking skills are explicitly taught and practiced in *Pathways Reading, Writing, and Critical Thinking*. Critical thinking—the ability to make judgments and decisions based on evidence and reason—is an essential skill for students in an academic setting, where they're expected to reflect on and analyze information rather than simply remember it. Students need to be prepared to think critically while listening, reading, writing, and participating in discussions.

The ability to think critically also contributes to language acquisition by requiring deep processing of the language. Having to consider an idea in relation to other ideas and then articulate a response or an opinion about it, involves making complex associations in the brain. This thought process in turn leads to better comprehension and retention of the target language.

Here are just a few examples of the academic tasks that require critical thinking skills:

- deciding which material from a reading to take notes on
- determining a writer's purpose when assessing the content of a reading
- forming an opinion on an issue based on facts and evidence
- relating new information to one's personal experiences
- giving specific examples to support one's main idea
- evaluating sources of information
- synthesizing information

The *Pathways* series gives explicit instruction and practice of critical thinking skills. Each unit has a Critical Thinking Focus and several practice exercises. For example:

D | Critical Thinking: Analyzing Similarities and Differences. In what ways are the structures you read about similar? In what ways are they different? Use your ideas from exercises **B** and **C.** Complete the Venn diagram.

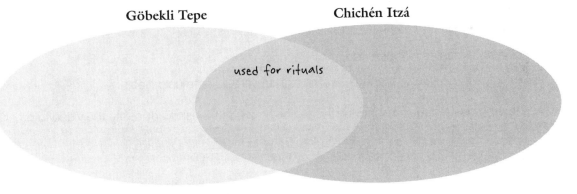

CT Focus

To identify **comparisons**, you need to scan for and select relevant details from different parts of the text, for example, names of people and places, years, dimensions, and other specific details.

Göbekli Tepe   Chichén Itzá

used for rituals

E | Critical Thinking: Synthesizing. In a small group, compare one of the structures from the reading with either La Sagrada Família or the Pyramids of Giza.

Using Video in the Language Classroom

The video clips in *Pathways Reading, Writing, and Critical Thinking* come from the award-winning *National Geographic* film collection and act as a bridge between Lessons A and B of each unit. The videos present another perspective on the unit theme in a visually dynamic way. The narration for each video has been carefully graded to feature vocabulary items and structures that are appropriate for students' proficiency level.

Teaching video-viewing skills

In daily life, nonfiction videos can be found on television, on the Internet, and in movie theaters in the form of documentaries. Just as *Pathways* provides a wide variety of reading passages to build students' reading skills, the series also builds viewing skills with videos from *National Geographic*. *Pathways* promotes visual and digital literacy so learners can competently use a wide range of modern media.

Videos differ from reading texts in important ways. First, students are processing information by viewing and listening simultaneously. Visual images include information about the video's setting as well as clues found in nonverbal communication, such as facial expressions, gestures, and other body language. The video may also include maps and diagrams to explain information and processes. The soundtrack contains narration, conversations, music, and sound effects. Some contextual words may appear on screen in signs or as identification of people or settings. In addition, full English subtitles are available as a teaching and learning option.

The Viewing section

The viewing section in each unit features activities for students to do before, while, and after they watch the video.

Before Viewing prepares students for the video by activating their background knowledge and stimulating interest in the topic. Some effective ways of previewing include

- brainstorming ideas and discussing what the class already knows about the topic;
- using photographs and the video's title to predict the content;
- pre-teaching key vocabulary essential to understanding the video content.

While Viewing tasks allow students to focus on

- checking their predictions;
- identifying the main ideas;
- watching and listening for particular details;
- watching and listening for opinions and inferences;
- observing gestures, body language, and other non-verbal communication.

After Viewing gives students opportunities to check comprehension and relate the video to other aspects of the unit by

- describing the main points or sequence of events;
- answering questions to check comprehension of main ideas and key information;
- synthesizing information from the video and previous reading material on the topic.

Some options for using the videos

Preview each video before presenting it in class to become familiar with the content, anticipate questions students might have, and plan how to exploit the video most effectively. See individual units in this Teacher's Guide for notes and suggestions for teaching each video.

Here are some techniques for using video in class:

- Have students preview the video by reading the transcript in the back of the student textbook.

- Pause, rewind, or fast-forward the video to focus on key segments or events.

- Pause the video and ask students to predict what will happen next. Resume the video so students can check their predictions.

- Have students watch the video, or parts of the video, with the sound off so they can focus on what they see. Have students share their ideas about the content. Then play the video with the sound on so students can check their ideas.

- After students have watched the video with the sound on, have them watch again with sound off. Pause the video in different places and ask students to retell the information in their own words.

- Have students watch first without subtitles and discuss the main ideas. Then play the video again with subtitles so students can check their ideas.

- Have students watch the video with the subtitles to help with unknown vocabulary and to aid comprehension.

- Have students watch the video independently and complete the activities in the Online Workbook.

As an optional special project, have students make a presentation or create a written report about a video of their choice, using language they have learned from the textbook and the video narration.

Video scripts are printed in the back of the student textbook. All video clips are on the Online Workbook, the Presentation Tool CD-ROM, and on the classroom DVD. The Online Workbook also contains additional activities about the video.

Features of the *Pathways* Teacher's Guides

The *Pathways* Teacher's Guides contain teaching notes, answer keys, reading and video overviews, and warm-up and extension activities to help teachers present the material in the student textbook.

Ideas for... Boxes

Throughout the *Pathways* Teacher's Guide, there are different types of *Ideas for. . .* Boxes:

- **Ideas for Presenting Grammar** provide a variety of ways to introduce grammatical structures and utilize the grammar charts presented in the Language for Writing sections of the textbook.

- **Ideas for Checking Comprehension** present additional questions for assessing students' comprehension of the reading texts.

- **Ideas for Expansion** suggest ways to expand on the content of the book when students need extra instruction or when they have a high level of interest in a topic.

- **Ideas for Further Research** provide suggestions for ways to explore the unit theme beyond the classroom.

Tips

Tips for instruction and classroom management are provided throughout the *Pathways* Teacher's Guide. The tips are especially helpful to less-experienced teachers, but they are also a resource for more-experienced teachers, providing new ideas and adding variety to the classroom routine.

Suggested Time Frames

The main sections of Lessons A, B, and C in the Teacher's Guide contain small clock icons with suggested times for completing the various tasks. The Writing Task sections in Lesson C do not have time icons because students will likely do writing assignments independently, outside of class. The times are intended as suggestions and may vary, depending on particular teaching situations. Similarly, the estimated time for completing a unit is between four and five class hours. This estimate may vary, depending on how much material is presented in class, given as homework, or other factors.

Graphic Organizers

A set of ten graphic organizers is included in the back of the Teacher's Guide (pages 101–110). You can photocopy these organizers as optional ways to help students organize information as they read particular reading texts in the units.

Audio Program

The audio program includes recordings of all the reading passages in the student textbook. As an option, you may have students listen to the texts while they read.

Following are some frequently asked questions about the *Pathways Reading, Writing, and Critical Thinking* series, answered by authors Mari Vargo and Laurie Blass.

1. How are the Student Book units organized?

Each unit in the *Pathways Reading, Writing, and Critical Thinking* series consists of three lessons: A, B, and C. Lessons A and B focus on reading, and Lesson C on writing. A video viewing segment between Lessons A and B serves as a bridge between the two readings and offers another perspective on the unit theme. Together, these lessons take students from an introduction to the unit theme, through a series of structured reading, vocabulary, and critical thinking activities, and finally through a guided writing assignment that synthesizes the skills, topics, and language presented in the unit.

2. What is the purpose of the Opening and Exploring the Theme pages?

The Opening page presents the unit goals—the Academic Pathways—and provides a general introduction to the unit theme through discussion questions. Exploring the Theme pages are springboards for students to interact with photographs and other graphical information such as maps, graphs, and charts. These pages get students thinking critically and sharing ideas about the unit theme. They present each unit's key concepts and vocabulary while providing opportunities for students to develop visual literacy skills.

3. How are the Lesson A and B readings different?

The Lesson A and B readings present academic content in a variety of genres and formats, and offer different perspectives on the unit themes. This content is adapted from a variety of *National Geographic* sources such as print and online features and articles.

The Lesson A readings are primarily single, linear texts. The Lesson B readings are usually a group of related shorter readings. They represent a variety of formats and text types, including news articles, Web pages, interviews, and profiles, that are linked to each other or to maps and other graphics. The linked aspect of the Lesson B reading texts mirrors a real-world, online reading experience.

4. How does *Pathways Reading, Writing, and Critical Thinking* develop reading strategies?

Each Lesson A presents an academic reading skill along with a series of practice activities. These skills include identifying main and supporting ideas, scanning for key details, understanding pronoun reference, understanding prefixes, recognizing noun clauses, and taking notes. Students apply what they have learned to the Lesson A reading and then have an opportunity to reinforce the skill in the Lesson B reading. In addition, Strategy boxes appear in various places throughout a unit, wherever students will benefit from a reminder of a previously taught skill.

5. How does the series develop critical thinking skills?

Critical thinking skills are explicitly taught and practiced in *Pathways Reading, Writing, and Critical Thinking*. Each Lesson A includes a specific CT (critical thinking) Focus box that explains the skill—often modeling the thinking process required by the skill through a series of questions. Critical thinking skills include analyzing fact and speculation, evaluating a writer's attitude, evaluating reasons and motivations, and making inferences. Students apply the skill to the reading passages in

Lessons A and B. Additional CT Focus boxes appear in other places in a unit, wherever students might benefit from a reminder of the skill.

In addition, there are multiple opportunities throughout each unit for students to practice synthesizing information—relating and connecting ideas from different parts of the unit—an essential skill for academic success. Students synthesize and apply information from the video and the Lesson A and B readings, which also prepares them for the unit's writing assignment.

6. How does the series build vocabulary skills?

A set of academic and high-frequency vocabulary items is targeted in both Lessons A and B. Students acquire and reinforce their knowledge of these items by identifying them in context, guessing their meaning, and using them in activities that reinforce meaning and usage. These target words are reinforced and recycled throughout the series.

In addition, Word Partners and Word Link boxes in Lessons A and B expand students' working vocabulary. Word Partners boxes show high-frequency patterns, or collocations, in which target words appear. Word Link boxes focus on prefixes, suffixes, and roots associated with target words.

7. What is the writing process approach taken in this series?

In acquiring academic writing skills, students need to learn early on that writing is re-writing. This is the premise of the process approach to writing, and the approach taken by *Pathways Reading, Writing, and Critical Thinking*. Accordingly, as students work through the pre-writing, writing, and post-writing activities in each unit, they draft

and re-draft their assignments. Repeating this process as they progress through the units, students internalize the steps and gradually become more independent writers.

8. How does it develop writing skills?

In *Pathways Reading, Writing, and Critical Thinking 1,* students are introduced to the writing process, and review and practice writing connected sentences on the unit topic, and then learn about and practice writing paragraphs. The writing section of each unit, Lesson C, begins with a presentation of the writing topic, and then proceeds through the writing process: gathering ideas, planning, drafting, revising, and editing. Students follow this process in a step-by-step manner, working through a series of structured activities. For example, they use outlines and graphic organizers in the planning stage, answer focused questions in the revision stage, and use a checklist in the editing stage.

Each Lesson C includes a Writing Skill presentation box along with a series of practice activities. These presentations include basic sentence-level writing skills such as using details to clarify ideas, and using synonyms to avoid repetition in the early units. Subsequent presentations include basic paragraph-writing skills such as writing topic sentences and supporting main ideas. Students practice by evaluating model sentences and paragraphs, and then apply what they've learned to their own writing as they write and revise their assignments.

In addition, each Lesson C includes a Language for Writing presentation that highlights a lexical or grammar point specifically useful for that unit's writing assignment. Examples include using the simple present of *be* and other verbs for describing routines and habits, and using modals *should, ought to,* and *could* for giving advice and making suggestions about becoming environmentally responsible. Students practice the structure in several activities, and then apply what they've learned to their own sentences and paragraphs as they write and edit their work.

9. What are some things to keep in mind when using the writing process?

In the brainstorming stage, students work with partners. This helps them express and clarify their ideas before they begin to write. In this stage, remind students that they should not monitor themselves or each other in any way. That is, ideas should flow freely without criticism or limitation.

The editing phase includes a peer evaluation activity that encourages students to give each other positive feedback at the outset. Reinforce the idea that students should read their partner's draft first just for meaning and to find at least one positive thing to say about the ideas in the sentences or paragraph. If

necessary, provide students with some positive conversation starters such as "I like the way you explain X." "Your idea about X is interesting." Remind them of some ways to soften suggestions, such as: "You might want to . . . " "You could . . . ."

10. How are reading and writing integrated in the series?

All the lessons in each unit of *Pathways Reading, Writing, and Critical Thinking* are thematically linked. Lesson A and B readings and activities present and reinforce ideas, vocabulary, and language that students will use in their Lesson C writing assignments. For example, in Unit 6, students learn to understand pronoun reference in the Lesson A passage, review the skill in Lesson B, and then focus on using pronouns to avoid repetition in their Lesson C sentences. In Unit 7, students read about explorers in both reading passages, then write about places they would like to explore.

Life in a Day

Academic Track: Interdisciplinary

Academic Pathways: Lesson A: Skimming for gist
                                    Guessing meaning from context
                  Lesson B: Reading interviews
                  Lesson C: Understanding the writing process
                                    Writing sentences about a single topic

Unit Theme

What happens in a single day on Earth? What kinds of living things can you find in a park in 24 hours? What is an average day like for three explorers?

Unit 1 explores the topic of what happens in a single day as it relates to:

– a film called *Life in a Day*
– a 24-hour BioBlitz of a park
– the daily lives of three explorers
– daily activities in students' lives

Think and Discuss *(page 1)*

5 mins

- Ask students to describe the picture. What does the picture make them think of? (Possible answers: Welcoming a new day at sunrise. Doing tai chi or yoga exercises.) Start a discussion by asking students if they have a special way to start each day. What is it?

- Discuss question 1 as a class. As a way to model and organize students' responses, you can create a T-chart. Draw a large capital *T* on the board. Under the left side, write *like best;* write *like least* on the right side. Go around the class and ask students for their answers. If some are repeated, put a checkmark next to them. (Note: Students may respond with a time of day such as "early morning" or with what they do at that time, e.g., "commuting to work.")

- For question 2, point out that students should choose someone with an unusual job or lifestyle. Ask volunteers to tell the class about the person they chose.

Exploring the Theme

15 mins

(pages 2–3)

The opening spread features five statistics about things that happen each day on Earth.

- Before students answer the questions, draw their attention to the explanation of numbers at the bottom of page 2. Point out that one billion has nine zeros, one million has six, and one thousand has three.

- Ask students for answers to the questions in Part A. What does the first question mean? (Answer: The number of people who are born is 200,000 more than those who die, so Earth's total population grows by 200,000 people daily.) Ask if anyone knows the Earth's total population. (Answer: It became greater than 7 billion in March 2012.) What two countries each have more than a billion people? (Answer: China and India.)

- Ask students to answer the questions in Part B about themselves. Have them share and compare their answers with a partner. Then lead a class discussion about questions 1–2.

- Ask about people moving from the countryside into cities. Do students know people who have done this? Why did the people choose to move to the city? (Possible answers: To find work. To be near their families. To attend college.)

Answer Key

A1. There are two hundred thousand more people on Earth each day. One billion children go to school, and three hundred million people use social networking sites.

A2. Answers will vary.

> **TIP**   For question B2, divide the class into groups and discuss which social networking sites they use, how often they use them, and what they use them for.

IDEAS FOR... Expansion

Ask students to find out more about the population in their countries. What are the figures for Internet and cell phone use each day? Which search words would help find this information on the Internet?

Preparing to Read *(page 4)*

30 mins

WARM-UP

The Lesson A target vocabulary is from a reading about the movie *Life in a Day*.

Ask students to imagine that they want to make a movie about different activities people around the world do in one day. They don't have money to travel around the world. How could they make the movie? Who might they ask to help? Write student ideas on the board. (Possible answers: They might ask family and friends to send videos. They might have a contest on the Internet. They might ask the government or a company for money.)

Exercise A. | Building Vocabulary

- Have students find the words in the reading and use the other words around them to guess their meanings. Then have students complete the sentences using one of the two words or phrases.

- Check the answers by asking volunteers to read out a sentence each.

- Point out the **Word Link** box. In general, students are encouraged to guess the meaning of words in context. However, using a dictionary to identify related words with the same root can be a good follow-up to build vocabulary.

Vocabulary Notes

People *communicate* when they share or exchange information. (Today, many people prefer to *communicate* electronically because it's quick and inexpensive.) Another phrase that means the same as *take care of* is *look after*. (Tanya *takes care of* her baby sister when her parents go out. She looks after her on Friday nights.)

TIP Review some of the clues that context words provide to identify the part of speech of target vocabulary items. For example, nouns are often preceded by an article such as *a* or *the*, as *team, result, globe,* and *project* are in the reading. Verbs sometimes take the infinitive form with *to*, as do *produce* and *communicate* in the passage. Adjectives frequently appear after a form of the verb *be* as *normal* and *connected* do in this reading.

Answer Key

1. globe	**5.** communicate	**9.** project
2. normal	**6.** arrive	**10.** produce
3. result	**7.** team	
4. connected	**8.** take care of	

IDEAS FOR... **Checking Comprehension**

Ask these questions or write them on the board.
1. How did people share their videos with Macdonald?
2. What are some examples of ordinary, normal activities in the movie?
3. What two questions did Macdonald's team ask the people? What were some of their answers?
4. Do you think people who see the film feel that they have a lot in common with the people in the videos? Explain.

Exercise B. | Using Vocabulary

Invite volunteers to share their answers with the class. (Possible answers: 1. email, telephone 2. mother, grandmother, nanny/babysitter 3. in sports or when working on a project)

Exercise C. | Brainstorming

- After students complete their answers individually, have them compare answers in pairs.

- Ask for volunteers to give their answers, and write them on the board.

Exercise D. | Scanning/Predicting

- Draw attention to the reading **Strategy** box. Students will apply this strategy to the reading.

- Explain that *predicting* is trying to guess the gist, or general idea, of the reading passage—what the most important idea is. Ask students to circle words or phrases that appear more than once on page 5. The words *life* and *day* appear by themselves as well as in the phrases *Life in a Day* and *single day*. Remind students that the plural of *life* is *lives*. Other words that are repeated are *team, videos,* and *movie*.

- Encourage students to look at the title of the reading as well as the pictures and captions. This will help them predict what the passage is about.

- Note: Students will check their predictions later, in exercise **A** on page 7.

track **1-01**

Ask students to read the passage. (Option: Have students listen to the audio as they read.) Explain that the vocabulary definitions in the footnotes at the bottom of pages 5 and 6 will help them understand the reading.

Overview of the Reading

The passage describes the making of the movie
Life in a Day. The project was based on videos that
people from all over the world contributed to describe
their lives on July 24, 2010. The film director, Kevin
Macdonald, also asked contributors to talk about what
they love most and what they fear. The main result of
the film was a sense of connectedness among people
throughout the world. You can view it on YouTube at
http://www.youtube.com/user/lifeinaday or learn
about the production of the movie at http://movies.
nationalgeographic.com/movies/life-in-a-day/

Understanding the Reading
(page 7)

15
ins

Exercise A. | Understanding the Gist

Check students' prediction in exercise **D** on page 4. Did
they guess the general idea correctly?

Answer Key

The correct answer is item c. The gist of the passage is
the making of the movie, but not a typical day in the life
of the director (a). There was nothing special or unusual
about the chosen day (b). The idea was to sample what
people do on a typical day.

Vocabulary Notes

In paragraph C, *banal* (rhymes with *canal*) means
"ordinary and commonplace to the point of being
boring."

Exercise B. | Identifying Key Details

- Explain that a statement must be completely true
  to be marked that way. False statements can be
  corrected with information from the passage so that
  they are true.
- For item 3, people uploaded 80,000 videos (not hours
  of videos). The total time was more than
  4,500 hours.

- After students complete the exercise, check answers
  as a class. Invite volunteers to say where they found
  the answers to the items.

Answer Key   1. T 2. T 3. F 4. T

Exercise C. | Critical Thinking: Guessing Meaning from Context

- Ask students to find and underline the six words in the
  reading, paying close attention to the words around
  them.
- Ask the class to look carefully at the words
  themselves and to think about word parts or words
  that are familiar. For example, *extraordinary* breaks
  into *extra*—something more—and *ordinary*—
  something usual. Although students may not know
  imaginary, they probably know the verb *imagine*
  and/or the noun *imagination*.
- Draw students' attention to the **CT Focus** box.
  Discuss why it is important to use context clues
  and not to rely on a dictionary. (Stopping to look up
  unfamiliar words slows down reading fluency and
  interferes with comprehension.)
- As students match the words with the definitions,
  have them try to substitute each definition in the
  passage to see if it fits and makes sense.
- Check answers as a class.

Answer Key

1. goes on (paragraph B)
2. imaginary (paragraph D)
3. extraordinary (paragraph C)
4. banal (paragraph C)
5. cultural (paragraph C)
6. contribute (paragraph E)

Exercise D. | Critical Thinking: Analyzing

Ask students to find details in the reading to support
their opinions.

Answer Key

Possible answers:
connected, aware of shared experiences, have a better
global understanding

Exercise E. | Personalizing

- Have students write their ideas individually and then
  compare their work in pairs.
- Discuss the questions as a class, comparing ideas.

Developing Reading Skills

45 mins *(page 8)*

Reading Skill: Skimming for Gist

- Make sure students understand that when we *skim,* we read quickly—to find the general idea of the passage.

- In real life, we skim frequently to decide whether a reading is useful to us. For example, if we are researching on the Internet, we may quickly skim many articles before finding one that suits our purpose.

- Explain to the class that when skimming a reading, it is useful to pay special attention to titles, subtitles, or headings, as well as to repeated words. Photos, captions, charts, and other graphics are also helpful in getting the gist of a reading.

track 1-02

Exercise A. | Skimming

- Ask students to read the lists of topics below paragraphs A and B. Then have them read the two paragraphs quickly, paying attention to the words in bold.

- Have students look again at the lists of topics and choose their answers.

Exercise B.

- Draw students' attention to the **CT Focus** box.

- Ask students to describe how they would guess the meaning of *rotate* in paragraph A. If necessary, point out that the word is defined in lines 5–6 (. . . rotate, or turn). Often a less familiar word is defined in context, sometimes set off with commas. Have students actively use the new words *rotate* and *rotation* by making a chart of how long it takes the different planets to make a complete rotation.

- Students now read the paragraph more slowly and in greater detail. This is a good opportunity to point out that we use different types of reading for different purposes. Before, students were skimming for gist; now, however, they will be paying closer attention to words and facts.

- When students finish reading the two paragraphs, find out through a show of hands how many students correctly identified the gist when skimming. How many chose the correct topic when reading the texts more carefully?

- Check comprehension by asking why topic 1 is the correct answer for both paragraphs. (In paragraph A, items 2 and 3 are details, not the main idea. In paragraph B, items 2 and 3 don't directly relate to the gist or main idea.)

Answer Key   **A.** 1 **B.** 1

Viewing: BioBlitz: Life in 24 Hours *(page 9)*

30 mins

Overview of the Video

An event called a BioBlitz was organized in Rock Creek Park, a park in Washington, D.C.

The video describes how this research project joined scientists and volunteers to count and identify every living thing in the park during a 24-hour period.

Rock Creek Park has a great deal of biodiversity. The main purpose of BioBlitz was to get people interested in the living things all around them.

National Geographic is helping to conduct yearly BioBlitzes in various parks. To learn more about the projects, go to http://www.nationalgeographic.com/explorers/projects/bioblitz/

Before Viewing

Exercise A. | Using a Dictionary

- Students become familiar with some of the key vocabulary in the video by using their dictionaries.

- Have students work in pairs to discuss the words and match them with their definitions.

- Compare answers as a class.

- Ask for volunteers to use each of the words in a new sentence.

Vocabulary Notes

The words vary from scientific (*biodiversity*) to informal (*stuff*). *Stuff* is used as a general word for an assortment of things. (Pete is moving to a smaller apartment, so he has to get rid of a lot of his *stuff*.) Check that the class understands that volunteers work without pay. Ask if any of them volunteer. If so, what kinds of organizations do they work for?

Answer Key

1. Stuff
2. behavior
3. Volunteers
4. Biodiversity
5. identify

Exercise B. | Brainstorming

After students have a chance to talk with a partner, ask pairs to tell the class about which plants, animals, and insects live in nearby parks. Offer help with vocabulary as necessary.

While Viewing

Exercise A.

- Ask students to read the questions.

- Play the video. Ask students to write short answers to the questions as they watch.

Answer Key

1. Find, count, catch, photograph, identify living things.
2. For only 24 hours.
3. It's in the middle of a large city and has a good amount of biodiversity.
4. To get people interested in the biodiversity that's all around them.

After Viewing

Exercise A.

- Have students work in pairs to discuss and compare answers.

- Play the video again and check answers.

Exercise B. | Critical Thinking: Synthesizing

- This may be some students' first encounter with a Venn diagram. Point out that the yellow and blue areas refer just to the movie or the BioBlitz event, but the overlapping green area in the center refers to both.

- Have students work individually to complete the diagram. Then have them compare answers in pairs. Finally, lead a class discussion to go over the answers. Encourage students to support their responses.

Answer Key

Life in a Day movie	Both	BioBlitz
4, 8	3, 5, 6, 7	1, 2

Preparing to Read

30 mins

(pages 10–11)

WARM-UP

Lesson B target vocabulary is presented in definitions, and students are then asked to use the new words to complete sentences.

Exercise A. | Building Vocabulary

- Ask students to choose if they want to work individually or in pairs.

- Explain that the words in blue are the new vocabulary words given with definitions. The task is to use the words appropriately to complete the sentences.

- Do the first item together with the class as an example.

- After checking the answer to item 5, draw students' attention to the **Word Link** box. Explain that learning prefixes like *un-* can help to expand vocabulary.

Answer Key

1. depends on   3. balance   5. unexpected
2. environment   4. during

IDEAS FOR... Expansion

For the **Word Link,** have a two-minute brainstorming activity where students work in small groups to think of as many words as possible that start with the *un-* prefix. When students share their lists, you may need to remind them that some words—like *under* and *uncle*—also start with *un-;* in these cases, however, the letters are part of the word and are not the negative prefix *un-*.

Exercise B. | Building Vocabulary

- In this second section, students must infer the meaning of the target vocabulary item from context and then match the word with a definition.

- Ask students to work in pairs to compare answers when they are finished.

Answer Key

1. measure   3. surprise   5. schedule
2. spend time   4. realize

Exercise C. | Using Vocabulary

- Point out the **Word Partners** box. Explain that some words often occur together with other words in speech and writing as in the examples here: *busy schedule, regular schedule*, etc. Explain that learning word partners can help students expand vocabulary. These word partners are sometimes called *collocations*.

- Remind students to respond to the questions with complete sentences.

- While students share their sentences with a partner, circulate through the classroom listening unobtrusively to students' interactions. Make sure that both partners participate equally.

Exercise D. | Predicting

- Draw students' attention to the **Strategy** box. The aim of this exercise is to create awareness of different genres of reading by making students familiar with structural features characteristic of that type of writing.

- Ask students: *What kinds of clues helped you answer the question?* The reading strategy of looking at titles, subheads, and photos will provide hints. The photos and subheads indicate that each of the three sections is about a different scientist. The title alerts readers to the main idea of the passage: a description of a typical day in the lives of the three individuals.

- Note: Students will check their predictions later, in exercise **A** on page 14.

track **1-03** Ask students to read pages 12 and 13. Explain that the vocabulary definition in the footnote at the bottom of page 13 will help students understand the reading.

IDEAS FOR... Expansion

For homework, ask students to find the play on words between Reading A and Reading B. Hint: Check the title of the movie described in Reading A and the title of the interviews in Reading B. (The first is *Life in a Day* and the second is *A Day in a Life.)* How are these the same and different?

Overview of the Reading

The interviews with three young explorers feature these aspects of their lives:

- a basic description of their jobs and where they work
- a typical workday
- their responses about the best and hardest aspects of their work
- an example of the strangest thing that has happened in their work (for two of them)

National Geographic conducts an Emerging Explorers program to identify and encourage promising young scientists from all over the world who are already showing potential at the beginning of their careers. These people are identified by senior scientists and are rewarded with $10,000 to help them with their research and exploration.

http://www.nationalgeographic.com/explorers/grants-programs/emerging-explorers/ has more information about the program and short descriptions of recent recipients, including the three in the reading.

Understanding the Reading

45 mins *(page 14)*

Exercise A. | Understanding the Gist

Check students' predictions in exercise **D** on page 11.

Answer Key

The answer is c. The general idea, or gist, of the article is descriptions of the daily lives of three scientific explorers.

Exercise B. | Identifying Key Details

- Explain that key details give more information about or examples of main ideas in a reading.
- In this three-circle Venn diagram, students decide whether a description applies to only one person (put the letter in the single-color circle under the person's name), two people (in the overlapping area between two individuals), or all three (in the dark orange area in the center of all three circles).
- Do items a and b as examples with the whole class. Then allow students time to work individually.
- Compare answers as a class.

Answer Key

Kakani Katija: b

Katsufumi Sato: c, j

h, i

a, g

Christine Lee: d, e, f

Exercise C. | Critical Thinking: Guessing Meaning from Context

- This is a three-step process. First, students find and underline the words in the passage. Second, they figure out what the words mean in context. Third, they match the words with their definitions.
- Ask students to work in pairs to locate and discuss the meaning of the words. Note that some words occur twice and that *engineers* appears in the caption for the photographs on page 12.
- After everyone has had a chance to complete the exercise, check answers as a class, asking students to support their answers with reference to the original use of the word in the reading passage.
- Make sure students understand that a *skull*—the bones of the head—is the top part of a skeleton.

Answer Key

1. buried	3. skeleton	5. dive
2. nocturnal	4. engineers	6. laboratory

Exercise D. | Synthesizing

Suggest that students look back at the readings to remember the main points. They may find it useful to review the script of the video on page 203 as well. The likely answer is that all three focus on what happens in a single day. Answers to the second set of questions will vary, but encourage students to support their opinions with details.

TIP Time permitting, you may want to have students work in pairs to recreate one of the interviews. The "interviewer" can ask the questions printed in bold and the "interviewee" can answer in their own words.

Exploring Written English

45 mins

(page 15)

In this lesson, students learn that writing—like reading—is not something that is done all at once. Just as there are stages of reading that lead to comprehension, there are stages in the writing process before a final draft is produced. The lesson starts with a review of the simple present and then presents the steps in the writing process. The process is then followed in producing sentences about daily activities.

Exercise A. | Language for Writing

- Go over the information in the box. It presents two important functions of the simple present: for habits and routines, and for facts or things that are generally true.

- This is a good opportunity to remind students about the Independent Student Handbook at the back of the Student Book. Page 214 reviews simple present verb forms.

- Likely areas for problems are the -s on third person singular verbs, the use of *doesn't* with the negative, and the forms of *be* and *have*.

- Have students complete the exercise. Check answers as a class.

Answer Key

1. communicate	4. doesn't work, works	7. ride
2. are	5. go, find	
3. is	6. have, has	

Exercise B.

- Have students work individually to write their own sentences for further practice with four verbs.

- Check answers by inviting volunteers to read their sentences aloud.

Exercise C.

- Students answer questions about themselves.

- As students work, circulate around the room and provide assistance as needed.

- Check students' work.

Exercise D.

- Students ask a partner the questions from exercise **C** and write answers in the third person singular form.

- Invite volunteers to share with the class any interesting information they learned about their partner.

IDEAS FOR... **Presenting Grammar**

For exercise **C,** write additional examples on the board of sentences with errors for students to correct. Students can also write their sentences from exercise **D** on the board for classmates to check.

Writing Skill: Understanding the Writing Process

- Go over the information in the box. Emphasize that good writing requires a series of steps. As you go over the stages, discuss which are done with other people and which are individual. Point out that, at first, it's more important to get ideas started than to focus on accuracy.

- If necessary, explain that journal writing is another strategy for generating ideas. Have you asked the class to acquire notebooks for journals? If not, you'll want to provide paper for this lesson.

- The term *graphic organizer* may not be familiar to all students. Explain that it's a visual way of showing the relationship of ideas from a text, such as the Venn diagrams in this unit.

Exercise E.

- Advise students to read the entire description before deciding on the correct stage.

- Check the answers as a class. Emphasize the flow of the process from coming up with ideas, organizing those ideas, and getting them down on paper.

Answer Key

1. drafting	3. revising	5. brainstorming
2. planning	4. editing	

Exercise F. | Critical Thinking: Evaluating

- Explain that the next step will be to put the process into action, so this is a good time for students to ask questions if anything is unclear.

- Students talk with a partner about the writing process stages and complete the sentences.

- Ask for volunteers to read their sentences aloud.

Writing Task: Drafting

(page 18)

Exercise A. | Brainstorming

- Remind students that brainstorming is a useful first step for gathering ideas before writing.

- Ask students to write words or phrases in their books or on a piece of paper. The focus is on generating ideas at this point. Some teachers find it helpful to set a time limit. Say, for example: *You have three minutes to think of all the things you do in a normal day. Just write them as fast as you think of them.*

Exercise B. | Planning

- Point out that at this stage, each student has a lot of flexibility in how to organize his or her ideas.

- Allow time for students to complete the chart individually.

- Ask volunteers to write their ideas on the board.

Exercise C. | Draft 1

- Remind the class that the main purpose of a first draft is to get ideas down on paper.

- As students write their sentences, walk around and offer help as needed. Refrain from any type of error correction at this point.

Writing Task: Revising and Editing *(page 19)*

Exercise D. | Peer Evaluation

- Explain that peer evaluation is a good way to get individualized feedback on your writing. All writers need to get feedback on their writing in order to improve.

- Discuss the three steps in the evaluation process to make sure students know what to do.

- Since this is the first time students will have done peer evaluation, give them some suggestions before they start. See question and answer 9 on page xiii of this book for ideas.

- Have students use the three questions to help them. Note that in question 3, there is no one "correct" order for ideas. Making sense is the most important thing.

- Ensure that both members of the pair have equal time to give feedback.

Exercise E. | Draft 2

- Walk around and monitor students as they work. Provide assistance as needed.

- Ask for volunteers to read their revised sentences aloud.

Exercise F. | Editing Practice

- The purpose of this exercise is to give students additional practice in editing for grammar in preparation for using the Editing Checklist for their second draft.

- Go over the information in the box.

- Allow time for students to find and correct the mistakes.

- Check the answers with the class by asking students to read out the correct sentences and explain the errors.

Answer Key

1. I **cook** food for 500 people every day.
2. I think most people **don't** cook for that many people.
3. My husband **drives** me to work every morning.
4. He **is** a bus driver.
5. I don't **work** in an office.
6. I **work** in a laboratory.
7. My wife and I **have** three daughters.
8. My daughter doesn't **have** a job.

Writing Task: Editing

(page 20)

TIP Some students may be surprised that sentences might need several revisions. Explain that even good writers often do several drafts of an essay. The first or second drafts usually focus on getting the ideas well organized and clearly presented. The final drafts usually focus on details such as spelling and punctuation.

Exercise G. | Editing Checklist

- Go over the sentences in the editing checklist.

- Allow time for students to read and edit their work.

- Ask students for some examples of each type of error.

Exercise H. | Final Draft

Have students complete their final draft, and then collect their work.

> **TIP** You can use students' sentences to collect (anonymous) examples of good sentences and common errors for the next class.

Unit Quiz

- Students can work in groups to answer the questions.
- Encourage students to refer back of the relevant pages of the unit to find the answers.
- To do the quiz as a competition, you can have students work in teams.

Answer Key

1. people	**5.** volunteers
2. loves and fears	**6.** schedule
3. Internet	**7.** environment
4. Skimming	**8.** revising

IDEAS FOR... Vocabulary Review

Ask students to create their own quiz based on vocabulary in this unit. Have students work in groups. Assign one reading or the video lesson to each group. Then have groups exchange quizzes and answer the questions without looking at the book. Alternatively, have each group select vocabulary items from anywhere in the unit.

IDEAS FOR... Further Research

Ask students to watch part of *Life in a Day*. They can take notes on things they find interesting or extraordinary and present their reports to the class in the next lesson.

Learning Experiences

Academic Track: Sociology/Education

Academic Pathways
Lesson A: Understanding the main ideas of paragraphs
Making inferences
Lesson B: Understanding news reports
Lesson C: Planning your writing
Writing sentences about goals

Unit Theme

Learning experiences vary globally with access to education, age, goals, and types of instruction.

Unit 2 explores the topic of learning as it relates to:

– literacy and school enrollment
– education for adults

– animal reasoning
– access to learning opportunities

Think and Discuss *(page 21)*

5 mins

- Ask students to describe the picture. Are the students working individually or in groups? How is the teacher helping the students? (Possible answers: They seem to be working in small groups. The teacher is pointing out something in a book, perhaps making a suggestion.) What are the other students doing? (Possible answer: They seem to be waiting their turn for the teacher to help them.)

- Discuss item 1 as a class. As a way to model and organize students' responses, draw a large, two-circle Venn diagram on the board with an overlap area in the middle. Write *in school* and *out of school* at the top of the circles and *both* in the overlap. Ask students what important things they've learned and where. (Possible answers: algebra [in school], riding a bicycle [out of school], using computers [in both places])

- Discuss question 2. Ask volunteers to tell the class the three most important things they learned in school. (Possible answers: reading, writing, counting, presenting projects, using a dictionary, etc.)

Exploring the Theme

15 mins *(pages 22–23)*

Featured on the spread are distribution maps showing global literacy rates and percentages of girls enrolled in primary school.

- Before students answer the questions, draw their attention to the map keys. Make sure they understand how to use the colors to interpret the information.

- Ask students to look at the first map and set of questions. Check their understanding of the words *literate* and *illiterate*, both of which are defined in context. Ask why literacy rates might be lower in some countries than in others.

- Ask students to look at the second map. *Primary school* is defined as "the early years of school." Ask the class what years primary school covers in their country.

- Be sure that students read the text above the maps. Lead a class discussion about the four questions, and discuss why illiteracy is greater for women than men. (Possible answer: In some cultures, literacy is not seen as important for girls as learning to care for a family and household.)

Answer Key

A1. There are high percentages of literate people in North and South America, Europe, Russia and China, Australia, and New Zealand.
A2. Places with many illiterate people are Central Africa, Yemen, Pakistan, and South Asia (India and Bangladesh).
B1. 96–100% of girls attend primary school.
B2. Fewer than 60% of young girls attend school.

TIP Have students work in small groups to ask each other questions about the maps. For example: Which country has more girls in primary school, the U.S. or Canada? (Answer: Canada) What does "no data" mean? Why might there be no data? (Answer: It means there is no information available—maybe because the countries don't keep records.)

IDEAS FOR... Expansion

Ask students to find out at what age students <u>must</u> start school in their country. At what age are students allowed to leave school? For example, in many places students are required to attend school from ages six to sixteen.

LESSON A

30 mins

Preparing to Read *(page 24)*

WARM-UP

The Lesson A target vocabulary is introduced in a matching exercise.

Ask students when most people learn to read and write. What are things that might prevent people from becoming literate as children? (Possible answers: Nowadays, most children learn to read and write at around age six. Wars or natural disasters often make it impossible for children to go to school; in remote areas, some children can't get to school because there is no public transportation.)

Exercise A. | Building Vocabulary

- Have students find the words in the reading and use the other words around them to guess their meanings. Then have them match the two parts of each sentence.
- Check the answers by asking volunteers to read out a sentence each.

Vocabulary Notes

Even native speakers confuse the homonyms *principal* (the head of a school) and *principle* (an idea about how people should behave). Help students remember the difference by pointing out that *princi**pal*** contains *pal* (an informal word for *friend*), indicating that the school principal could be thought of as a friend.

> **TIP** Ask where students have seen a word related to *ordinary* in Unit 1. The first reading contained the word *extraordinary*, defined on page 7. Ask the class for examples of things that are ordinary and extraordinary. For example, a full moon is ordinary, but an eclipse is extraordinary.

Answer Key

1. e 2. d 3. a 4. b 5. c

Exercise B. | Building Vocabulary

- Have students find the blue words in the reading and use the other words around them to guess their meanings. Then have them complete the sentences with the words in the box.
- Check the answers by asking volunteers to read out a sentence each.
- Point out the **Word Link** box with the prefix *in-,* which like the prefix *un-* featured on page 10, means "not." Explore the effect of *in-* with the words *dependent* and *independent*. Ask for examples of each adjective as they relate to people at different stages of life. For example, typically, children and elderly people are more likely to be dependent than young and middle-aged adults, who are usually more independent.

Exercise C. | Using Vocabulary

- Allow time for students to work in pairs to discuss the questions.
- Invite volunteers to share their answers with the class.

Exercise D. | Brainstorming

- In the Writing section of Unit 1, students were introduced to brainstorming as a way to quickly come up with a lot of ideas. Remind them that when they brainstorm, ideas are more important than spelling or grammar.
- Allow time for students to complete the exercise individually and then compare answers in pairs.
- Students may focus on subject matter, but educators think that the "soft skills" children develop at school are important, too. These include working cooperatively with others, taking turns, and learning when to work independently.

Exercise E. | Scanning/Predicting

- Draw attention to the reading **Strategy** box. Explain that *scanning* means reading the passage very quickly to find specific information. Therefore, it is not necessary to read the passage thoroughly or to continue reading once the information has been found.
- Get students in the habit of figuring out what kinds of clues will help them find the answer. The **Strategy** box helpfully suggests looking for capitalized proper names for this scanning task.
- Remind the class that predicting is trying to guess the gist, or general idea, of the reading passage.
- Ask students to use the title, subheads, and first page to predict what the reading is about. Also encourage students to use photographs and captions to make their predictions.
- Note: Students will check their predictions later, in exercise **A** on page 27.

track 1-04 Ask students to read the passage. Explain that the vocabulary definitions in the footnotes at the bottom of pages 25 and 26 will help them understand the reading.

> **IDEAS FOR...** **Expansion**
>
> Ask students to add the new target vocabulary to their notebooks. Encourage them to be aware of these words as they encounter them in daily life. When they read or hear one of these words, they should make a brief note of how it was used. Once a week, allow time for students to share their new words with the class.

Overview of the Reading

The passage is about an elderly Kenyan farmer who heard a radio announcement about free primary school education. When Kimani Maruge was young, his family couldn't afford schooling, so he was illiterate. When he learned about the new government policy at age 84, Maruge decided to attend primary school and become literate. Although he had to overcome many obstacles, Maruge persisted in learning and worked to help other Kenyans become educated.

In 2010, a film entitled *The First Grader* was made about Maruge's story. The movie has inspired other Kenyan adults to become literate.

Read a synopsis of the film at **http://www.imdb.com/ title/tt0790663/synopsis** or watch an introduction to the movie at **http://video.nationalgeographic.com/ video/movies/thefirstgrader/first-grader-trailer/**

Understanding the Reading
(page 27)

45 mins

Exercise A. | Understanding the Gist
Check students' predictions in exercise **E** on page 24. Did they guess the general idea correctly?

Answer Key

Name: Kimani Maruge, Country: Kenya

The correct answer is b because at the age of 84, Kimani Maruge was a highly unusual student. Items a and c are not correct because there is no mention of an unusual parent or an unusual teacher.

Exercise B. | Identifying Key Details
- Students use information from the reading passage to complete the sentences.
- When you go over the answers as a class, be sure to accept paraphrased answers that are correct.

Answer Key

1. 84
2. free
3. principal
4. fighting and burning houses
5. education
6. go to school/learn to read

Exercise C. | Critical Thinking: Analyzing/ Inferring
- Before students can decide whether descriptions apply to Maruge or not, they need to understand the adjectives. Review the words students have learned earlier in the unit. Encourage them to use a dictionary, if necessary, to find the meanings of the other adjectives.
- Check the answers as a class.

Answer Key

2. *Ordinary* doesn't describe Maruge, a very unusual man.
3. *persistent* should be checked because Maruge went as far as seventh grade; he attended school during difficult times, and even when he lived in a home for the elderly.
4. *hardworking* describes Maruge because he was a successful student who studied Swahili, English, and math.
5. *caring* should be checked because Maruge taught other residents and asked for help to educate people in Kenya when he was at the United Nations.
6. *brave* describes Maruge because he fought colonialism and because he continued to study during times of fighting.

Vocabulary Notes
- *Character traits* are descriptions of general aspects of a person's behavior and personality. They are usually adjectives that have a positive or negative sense, or *connotation*.
- If students are unfamiliar with the concept of character traits, provide examples on the board and have the class discuss whether the traits are positive or negative.

Exercise D. | Critical Thinking: Making Inferences
- Sometimes information about a person's character is explicitly stated in the reading passage. For example, the first sentence in paragraph D states that Maruge was motivated. However, frequently students have to use information to *infer* or indirectly reason what a person's character is like.
- Draw students' attention to the **CT Focus** box.
- Check that students understand the meaning of *motivation* (a reason to do something). Ask them to work in pairs to go through the reading, looking for Maruge's actions and possible motivations for why he acted as he did.

Answer Key

Possible answers:

1. He valued education and understood the importance of being able to read and write.
2. He was motivated to read the Bible and study veterinary medicine.
3. He knew he was an international figure and that people would pay attention to what he said.

Exercise E. | Personalizing

Lead a class discussion about what the two sayings mean, and have students say why they agree more with one or the other. The sayings express opposite viewpoints: The first suggests that a person can learn at any age, while the second implies that an old person can't learn new things.

IDEAS FOR...   Expansion

For homework, ask students to write five character traits they think describe them, giving an example of actions for each one. They should write these on a piece of paper without giving their name or other identification. At the start of the next class, ask students to work in groups of four and combine and mix their papers. One person should read each description while the others try to guess who it is.

Developing Reading Skills *(page 28)*

Reading Skill: Understanding the Main Ideas of Paragraphs

- Check to make sure everyone understands what a *paragraph* is. (Answer: a piece of writing that has one main idea supported by examples or details)

- Point out that the main idea often appears in the first sentence of a paragraph. In that case, that first sentence is the paragraph's *topic sentence*.

- Have students look through the paragraph to find signal words that are used with supporting details. (Answers: for example, reasons, as a result, for these reasons)

track 1-05

Exercise A. | Understanding the Main Idea

In this case, the main idea appears in the first sentence of the paragraph. Note that the main idea is repeated in the concluding sentence.

Answer Key

It's a good idea for older adults and children to attend school together.

Exercise B. | Identifying the Main Idea

- Students get additional practice in identifying the main idea of a paragraph by revisiting paragraph D of the reading passage.

- Ask volunteers for suggestions for the main idea.

Answer Key

Maruge was a successful student.

Exercise C. | Matching

- Students now reread four other paragraphs from the reading passage, looking for the main idea of each.

- Have students compare answers with a partner before going over them as a class.

Answer Key

1. G 2. C 3. A 4. E

30 mins

Viewing: Alex the Parrot
(page 29)

Overview of the Video

The video describes how cognitive biologist Dr. Irene Pepperberg interacted with her parrot, Alex, who seemed able to identify objects and tell about the relationships between them. For example, Alex could identify which things were larger or smaller than other things, as well as count items and distinguish different colors.

Dr. Pepperberg believes these skills demonstrate that birds like Alex have cognitive skills that enable them to reason instead of simply mimic, or copy, actions. However, not all scientists agree with the results of Pepperberg's 30-year study with Alex. They think that the parrot may have picked up cues from his environment when he answered questions.

To read an article that is sympathetic to Pepperberg's research as well as other studies of animal cognitive behavior, see http://ngm.nationalgeographic.com/2008/03/animal-minds/virginia-morell-text

Before Viewing

Exercise A. | Using a Dictionary

- Students become familiar with some of the key vocabulary in the video by looking up the words in the box and matching them with the definitions.
- Compare answers as a class.
- Ask for volunteers to use each of the words in a new sentence.

Vocabulary Notes

When you *mimic* something, you imitate it without processing information. That's how people thought parrots were able to talk before the studies with Alex. By contrast, when you *reason,* you process information before coming to a conclusion or giving an answer. Ask the class if they know of any intelligent animals that seem to be able to reason. Ask for volunteers to give examples.

Answer Key

1. reasoning 2. mimic 3. cognitive 4. specific

Exercise B. | Thinking Ahead

When students have had a chance to talk with a partner, ask pairs to give their opinions about whether parrots understand what they are saying. After watching the video, come back to this point and see if students still have the same point of view.

While Viewing

Exercise A.

- Ask students to read the questions.
- Play the video while students take notes.

Answer Key

1. F (Because many parrots can talk. Alex amazed scientists because he apparently knew what he was talking about.)
2. T
3. T
4. F (Alex learned 150 words.)

After Viewing

Exercise A.

- Have students discuss and compare answers with a partner.
- Students should correct the false sentences with information from the video.
- If necessary, play the video again to check answers.

Exercise B. | Synthesizing

Remind students that they learned the word *extraordinary* in Unit 1. When people synthesize, they combine information from two or more different sources to create something new. Encourage students to think about what they read in Lesson A and saw in the video to come up with new insights based on the fact that both Kimani Maruge and Alex were extraordinary, although in very different ways.

Answer Key

Possible answers:
Alex was extraordinary because of his ability to reason and understand concepts. Maruge was extraordinary because late in life he decided to become literate.

Preparing to Read

(pages 30–31)

WARM-UP

The Lesson B target vocabulary is presented in sentences about education and different cultures.

Exercise A. | Building Vocabulary

- Do the first item together with the class as an example. Ask for other sentences using the noun *aid*.

- Point out the **Word Usage** box, which discusses the two different pronunciations of *record* depending on its part of speech. As a noun, a *record* is a written piece of evidence about something. When *record* is used as a verb, it means "to make a permanent copy of something."

Answer Key

1. a **2.** b **3.** a **4.** b **5.** b **6.** a **7.** a **8.** a **9.** a **10.** b

---

IDEAS FOR... **Expansion**

For the **Word Usage**, go over the two meanings of *record*, using examples such as a birth or marriage certificate as a *record* and YouTube videos of examples of people recording music or actions. Ask students for other examples.

Exercise B. | Using Vocabulary

- Direct students' attention to the **Word Partners** box, where words often used together with *trip* are given. Elicit other words that are often found with *trip*. (Possible answers: round trip, day trip, shopping trip)

- Remind students to respond to the questions with complete sentences.

- While students share their sentences with a partner, circulate through the classroom listening unobtrusively to students' interactions.

Answer Key

Answers will vary, but possible answers for item 1 would mention the name of a destination and a purpose for traveling. For item 2, possible skills are the ability to learn languages and patience!

IDEAS FOR... **Expansion**

Build on question 3 as a way of heightening students' awareness of related languages, something students will encounter in the next reading. Ask if they know about language families—groups of languages that are closely related in a number of ways. Use Scandinavian languages Norwegian, Danish, and Swedish or perhaps Romance languages Italian, Spanish, Portuguese, etc., as examples.

Exercise C. | Scanning/Predicting

- Point out the **Strategy** box and remind students of the value of looking for capitalized proper nouns. Suggest that students circle the place names as they find them and then come back to the exercise and check their circled names against the list.

- Before you ask about students' predictions, draw their attention to the title of the passage. What does *global* mean? (Answer: worldwide) What is the subtitle of the passage? (Answer: News Stories from the World of Learning)

track **1-06** Have students read the three news stories. Explain that the footnote at the bottom of page 33 will help them understand the reading.

TIP When giving students feedback on exercise C, encourage their peers to explain why some capitalized place names are not countries. Students may have carefully followed the Strategy but ended up with other names that do not appear on the list because they are names of islands, states, cities, or tribal groups.

Overview of the Reading

The simulated news stories describe four case studies in expanding educational opportunities. The experiments involved:

- a tribe in Indonesia with an unwritten language using a Korean alphabet to record the sounds of their language

- a youth worker in Los Angeles, U.S., getting city students outdoors to build their skills

- mobile libraries in Ethiopia delivering books to children in remote areas

- tent schools traveling with nomadic families in Mongolia

National Geographic has a special Education site to help teachers, families, and students develop geoliteracy and awareness of news events from around the world. The home page of the site features two Quick Find resources for looking up information by topic or keywords. As a teacher, think about how you could use the site with your students as you explore its many features.

Go to: http://education.nationalgeographic.com/education/reference-and-news/?ar_a=1

Understanding the Reading *(page 34)*

Exercise A. | Understanding the Gist

Check students' predictions in exercise **C** on page 31.

Answer Key

Countries: Indonesia, the United States, Korea, Ethiopia, Mongolia

The main idea is 3. Item 1 is not correct because only the first case study deals with language learning and that is mostly in the context of preserving an unwritten language. While it is true that the second case study features learning about the natural world (2), the concept is not the general idea or gist of the whole reading passage.

Exercise B. | Identifying Main Ideas

- Explain that each sentence refers to one lettered paragraph of the reading.
- Ask students how they usually go about finding the main idea. If necessary, tell them to look back at page 28.
- Do the first item as an example. Then allow students time to work individually.
- Compare answers as a class.

Answer Key

Main ideas are given for paragraphs A, E, F, and H. The main idea for paragraph B is that the Hangul alphabet can be used to write the sounds of Cia Cia. The main idea for paragraph I is that tent schools move with nomadic families in Mongolia.

Exercise C. | Identifying Key Details

- Explain that key details give examples or more information about main ideas in a reading.
- Do the first item as an example.
- Ask students to work individually at first. Then they should compare answers in pairs, explaining to each other why some statements are false.

Answer Key

1. T **2.** F (Cia Cia is not written.) **3.** F (He grew up in Los Angeles.) **4.** T **5.** T

Exercise D. | Critical Thinking: Inferring/ Synthesizing

- Encourage students to look back at the readings to remember the main points.
- As they did at the end of the video, students are again going to use information from two different sources together in a new way.
- For the first item, draw a T-chart on the board and put similarities on one side and differences on the other.
- Ask students to work in small groups of three or four to discuss how the two individuals are similar and different.
- Encourage a representative from each group to go to the board and write ideas in the two categories.
- When all groups have finished, discuss the chart on the board as a class. If individuals or groups disagree, ask them to support their ideas with examples.

Answer Key

Possible answers:

Similarities: Both men grew up poor, and both understand and appreciate the importance of education. Also, both men helped other people change their lives.

Differences: Martinez had a life-changing experience as a young man, but Maruge was 84 before he started school. The way they reached out to other people was different, too.

Exploring Written English
45 mins
(pages 35–37)

In this lesson, students go through the process of writing sentences about an educational goal and how they plan to achieve it. The lesson starts with a comparison of the use of the verbs *want* and *need*.

Exercise A.

- Go over the information in the Language for Writing box. *Want* is presented as something you would <u>like</u> to do, while *need* is used for things you <u>must</u> do.

- Ask students to work individually to unscramble the sentences and then compare answers in pairs.

- Check the answers as a class.

Answer Key

1. Some older Kenyans want to go to school.
2. We need to take an exam this month.
3. Ethiopia Reads wants to build more libraries in Ethiopia.
4. The Cia Cia tribe needs to find a writing system.
5. The students want to learn about the environment.

Exercise B.

- Go over the example with the class. Make sure students understand why *needs* is the correct answer.

- Allow time for students to circle their answers individually.

- Monitor students as they work, and identify problem areas.

- Give general feedback on common problems that you found.

Answer Key

1. need 2. want 3. need 4. need

Exercise C.

- Explain the first part of the task: Students write about things they want and need to do in the next five years.

- As students work, circulate around the room and offer help as needed.

- After students have completed their chart, tell them to compare it with a partner's chart and use it to ask and respond to questions.

- When students have written their four sentences, invite volunteers to read their sentences aloud.

Exercises D and E.

- Go over the information in the Writing Skill box.

- Explain the task in exercise **D**, and answer any questions that arise. Note that a set of steps or a process is typically used to describe *needs*. By contrast, *wants* are often based on reasons, which can be organized by prioritizing the most important ones.

- Allow time for students to complete the tasks either individually or in pairs.

- Check answers with the class.

Answer Key

b, a
a. 5, 1, 4, 2, 3
b. Answers will vary.

IDEAS FOR... Planning Your Writing

After exercise **E**, ask students about the steps they need to take in order to choose a major field of study. Where do they start? What is the next step and the following one? What is the final step, and why does it come last?

Writing Task: Drafting
(page 38)

Exercise A. | Brainstorming

- Remind students that brainstorming is a useful first step for gathering ideas before writing.

- Explain the task, making sure that students understand the word *goal* (an objective or a purpose).

- Ask students to write down words or phrases about their educational goals. The focus is on fluency and generating ideas at this point. Some teachers find it helpful to set a time limit. For example: *You have three minutes to think of all the things you want to learn in the next couple of years. Just write them down as fast as you think of them.*

- Where do students want to pursue their goals and what do they need to do? Places can vary from institutions to parts of the world, and needs can range from money or a scholarship to physical equipment for their project. Tell the students to complete the chart.

Exercise B. | Planning

- Go over the steps in this exercise.
- Allow time for students to work individually.
- Walk around and monitor students as they work. Provide assistance as needed.

Exercise C. | Draft 1

- Remind the class that a first draft is simply getting ideas down on paper.
- As students write their sentences, walk around and offer help. Refrain from any type of error correction at this point.

Writing Task: Revising and Editing *(page 39)*

Exercise D. | Peer Evaluation

- Remind students that peer evaluation is intended to help them understand what makes sentences clear and well organized.
- Go over the five steps and tell students to use them to comment on their partner's work.
- Ensure that both members of each pair have equal time to give feedback.

Exercise E. | Draft 2

- Walk around and monitor students as they work. Provide assistance as needed.
- Remind students to use the feedback they got from their partner.

Exercise F. | Editing Practice

- Explain the importance of editing in good writing.
- Go over the points in the box.
- Allow time for students to find and correct the errors in the sentences.
- Check the answers by asking volunteers to read out the corrected sentences and explain the errors.

Answer Key

1. You need **to get** a passport before you can study in Canada.
2. The student **needs** to take an entrance exam when he applies to college.
3. The organization wants **to build** more libraries in Ethiopia.
4. Maruge went to primary school because he wanted **to learn** to read.
5. The Cia Cia want **to save** their language for future generations.

Writing Task: Editing *(page 40)*

TIP Students may be surprised that sentences might need several revisions. Explain that even good writers often produce several drafts of an essay. The first or second drafts usually focus on getting the ideas well organized and clearly presented. Final drafts usually focus on details such as spelling and punctuation.

Exercise G. | Editing Checklist

- Go over the sentences in the editing checklist.
- Allow time for students to read and edit their work.
- When students finish editing their work, ask for some examples of each type of error in the list.

Exercise H. | Final Draft

Have students complete their final draft, and then collect their work.

TIP You may want to suggest that students keep copies of their drafts in a portfolio so that they can see how their writing develops over the course of several drafts.

Unit Quiz

- Students can work in groups to answer the questions.
- Encourage students to refer back to the relevant pages of the unit to find the answers.
- To do the quiz as a competition, you can have students work in teams.

Answer Key

1. Literacy
2. independent
3. the importance of education
4. main idea
5. color
6. similar to
7. Ethiopia, Mongolia
8. need

IDEAS FOR...   Grammar Review

Ask students to create a poster about things that they might want to do to be successful in their academic programs and then things they must do. Have them provide suggestions for how they could achieve the things they want to do.

IDEAS FOR...   Further Research

Ask students to find out about lifelong learning by researching the two keywords on the Internet. At one time, people thought that education was "complete" or "finished" when they graduated from college, but rapid changes in technology have made it necessary for people to constantly continue learning in order to keep up with world events. Is lifelong learning supported in the country where students now live? If so, how is it done? (For example, the U3A, or University of the Third Age, program functions worldwide through the Internet.)

Family Ties

Academic Track: History/Anthropology

Academic Pathways: Lesson A: Finding the right meaning
                                   Identifying fact and speculation
                         Lesson B: Synthesizing map and textual information
                         Lesson C: Expressing speculation
                                     Writing descriptive sentences about family

Unit Theme

Families are connected over the generations between ancestors and descendants. DNA analysis identifies ancestors from thousands of years ago and shows how all humans are related.

Unit 3 explores the topic of family as it relates to:

– genealogy
– the Genographic Project

– family histories
– major human migration routes

Think and Discuss *(page 41)*

5 mins

- Ask students how parents transport or carry babies in the their culture(s). (Possible answers: In their arms, on their backs, in special equipment such as carriages or strollers) Start a discussion by asking students why babies are carried in this way. (Possible answer: A mother carries her baby on her back as she goes about her work as in the second photo on page 42.)

- Discuss question 1 as a class. Ask how many students actually know/knew their grandparents or great-grandparents (their parents' grandparents). How old are/were these people? Do/Did they live with the family, alone, or in special residences?

- Discuss question 2. Ask volunteers to tell the class how they have information about their family history

Exploring the Theme

15 mins

(pages 42–43)

The opening spread features photographs of families from around the world, with a number indicating how many generations are represented in each picture.

- Before students answer the questions, ask them to quickly skim the text for gist with special attention to the words *generation* and *genealogy.*

- Ask students to work with a partner as they explore the photographs and captions. For each photo, they should try to identify the generations. What clues help to tell how the people are related?

- Students work in pairs to answer the first two questions. Then discuss the questions with the class.

- Ask students to answer question 3 about their own families. Have them share and compare their answers with a partner.

Answer Key

1. Genealogy is the study of family history. People usually start with older members of their families, asking about memories or stories from the past. Research continues by finding records about births, marriages, and deaths as well as information about where people lived and worked. Today, there are many websites and software programs to help gather and display information.
2. Answers will vary. Encourage students to give reasons for their opinions.
3. Answers will vary.

TIP Ask students what ages their own generation includes. Sometimes members of the same generation develop a reputation for being alike and therefore companies try to market certain kinds of goods to them. For example, in the U.S., Generation X consists of people born in the 1960s and 1970s. Ask if the students' generation gets targeted by certain kinds of advertising. What kind and why?

IDEAS FOR... Expansion

Ask students to go online using the keyword *genealogy* to explore some of the many sites that might help them find out about their family history. Caution students that they should not get involved with any sites that require payment.

Preparing to Read *(page 44)*

30 mins

WARM-UP

The Lesson A target vocabulary is introduced in a matching and a sentence-completion exercise.

Ask students what they know about DNA, the inherited material that carries genetic information in the cells of every living thing. Lead a class discussion about the many ways analysis of DNA can be valuable.

Exercise A. | Building Vocabulary

- Have students find the blue words in the reading and circle those that they are not sure about. Then tell them to use the other words around the unfamiliar words to guess their meanings. Finally, have them match the two parts of the sentences.

- Check the answers by asking volunteers to read out a sentence each.

TIP Making associations with words students already know is a good strategy for learning new words and making them meaningful. One approach is to think of opposites such as *ancient* and *recent* or *modern*. A *major* problem may cause difficulties, but a *minor* problem is easily solved.

Answer Key

1. a 2. c 3. d 4. e 5. b

Exercise B. | Building Vocabulary

- Point out the **Word Link** box. The root *migr* is found in two of the target vocabulary words: *immigrant* and *migrate*.

- Ask students to suggest definitions for each of the additional words. Have students use their dictionaries for any words they can't figure out.

- Draw students' attention to the words in the box. After students locate the words in the passage and guess their meaning from context, they complete sentences with them.

- Check answers as a class.

Answer Key

1. Information 2. section 3. recent 4. migrate
5. trace

Exercise C. | Using Vocabulary

- After students complete their answers individually, have them compare answers in pairs.

- Invite volunteers to share their answers with the class.

Answer Key

Students' answers will vary, but for question 2, collecting oral histories from elderly living relatives can be a good place to start. Another useful source is records such as birth, marriage, and death certificates.

TIP Unless students are aware of genetic analysis for genealogy, question 3 may not produce answers. You may want to leave it for now and come back to this point after the students have seen the video. By then, students will know more about the possibilities.

Exercise D. | Brainstorming

- By now, students know that brainstorming is a way to quickly come up with ideas. Continue to remind students that when they brainstorm, ideas are more important than spelling or grammar.

- Have students work in pairs to brainstorm. As you move around the classroom, check that both members of each pair are contributing ideas to the process.

Answer Key

Possible answers:
where they came from, when they were born, when they died, their full names, their children's names, when they migrated, their occupations

Exercise E. | Scanning/Predicting

- Students are going to review scanning for capitalized proper nouns: the name of Spencer Wells and a place name. Once they find these names, they need to identify who Wells is and what he is doing. (Answer: Wells is the director of a large project sponsored by National Geographic. The project collects DNA from cheek swabs and blood samples to learn more about ancient humans and how they migrated.)

- There may be some confusion about the place until students learn that Queens is one borough, or section, of New York City and that Astoria is a neighborhood in Queens.

- The question about what Wells is doing can elicit answers ranging from immediate details (collecting cheek swabs) to the large-scale project about ancient human migration.

- Note: Students will check their predictions later, in exercise **A** on page 47.

Ask students to read the passage. Explain that the vocabulary definitions in the footnotes at the bottom of page 45 will help them understand the reading.

IDEAS FOR... **Expansion**

If students seem interested in their own ancestry, suggest that they make a chart or family tree showing all the ancestors they can think of. If they live far from home, they could send the chart to their families as a way of getting them interested, too, and perhaps starting a family-history project.

Overview of the Reading

The passage describes the visit of the director of National Geographic's Genographic Project to an ethnically varied neighborhood in New York City. The project uses DNA samples to trace human movements and interrelationships in the distant past. Human DNA has certain markers or distinct patterns that are passed from one generation to the next. Different populations have different markers, so geneticists use these to identify a person's heritage within general migration streams in human history.

To learn more about National Geographic's Genographic Project, visit the site at **https://genographic. nationalgeographic.com/genographic/index.html**

IDEAS FOR... **Checking Visual Literacy**

The reading passage on pages 45 and 46 contains a map, photographs, and a colored timeline. Go over these points with the class after students have had a chance to work through the reading independently.

1. Note the gray dates above the chart ranging from 120,000 years ago on the far left to the present on the right.
2. On the right side of the timeline is a key to the colors used for different parts of the world. Note that these colors are the same as the ones on the map. Ask what color is used for the following places: East Africa, South America, Southeast Asia, Northern Europe.
3. The study had 193 volunteers, and the thickness of the colors corresponds to the number of volunteers with ancestors from that region. Ask what regions had the most and the fewest ancestors.
4. Point out the lines from the right of the chart up to the photographs. Also notice that the names of the four people are given on the map. Ask about the routes on the map and how they relate to each of the four people.

Understanding the Reading *(page 47)*

45 mins

Exercise A. | Understanding the Gist

Check students' predictions in exercise **E** on page 44. Did they guess the general idea correctly?

Answer Key

1. Spencer Wells is the director of the Genographic Project.
2. He's in Astoria, Queens, New York City.
3. He's collecting cheek swabs and blood samples to help trace the history of human migration.

Exercise B. | Identifying Main Ideas

- Have students work individually to complete the task and then compare answers with a partner.
- Point out that although the main idea often appears in the first sentence of a paragraph, in this exercise, the main idea can be found in the last sentence.

Answer Key

1. b 2. a

Exercise C. | Identifying Key Details

- Students use information from the graphics and text on page 46 to match statements to the four people.
- Encourage students to use the colored arrows at the right of the chart together with the routes on the map to answer items 1, 2, and 4. For item 3, it is necessary to use the time scale at the top of the chart. Pedro's ancestors left the Middle East sometime between 40,000 and 35,000 years ago to move through Central Asia and Siberia before migrating to the Americas.

Exercise D. | Critical Thinking: Fact vs. Speculation

- Draw students' attention to the exercise title and ask if anyone knows the meaning of the word *speculation*. (Answer: You speculate when you guess or form an opinion without having all the facts.) Tell students to read the **CT Focus** box carefully, making note of the kinds of indefinite words that are commonly used with speculations.
- As students work in pairs, have them circle the words in items 1–4 that told them the sentences were expressing speculation and not fact. (Answers: 2. could 4. probably)
- Check answers as a class.

Answer Key

1. F 2. S 3. F 4. S

Exercise E. | Personalizing

When students finish writing their question, have them share it with a partner. Then ask for volunteers to read their questions aloud.

Developing Reading Skills *(page 48)*

45 mins

Reading Skill: Finding the Right Meaning

- Go over the information in the box.
- Review the major parts of speech by asking volunteers for examples of nouns, verbs, adjectives, and adverbs.

Exercise A. | Matching Definitions

- After students complete the exercise individually, have them compare answers in pairs.
- Check answers with the class.

Answer Key

cell: 2, 1; branch: 2, 1, 3

Exercise B. | Finding Definitions

- Explain the task: Students are given three words with their part of speech and asked to provide two definitions and sample sentences for each of the words.
- Note: This may be a good homework assignment. At the start of the next class, go over the definitions and sentences, asking for several examples of each word.

Answer Key

Students' sample sentences will vary, but definitions may include:

cross: to go over or across something; to pass while going in opposite directions; to oppose or anger someone

trace: to follow something to its origins; to copy onto thin paper from an image underneath

direction: a route or geographic line of movement; leadership or guidance toward goals; artistic management and control; an approach or line of thought; an instruction (usually used in the plural)

30 mins

Viewing: The World in a Station *(page 49)*

Overview of the Video

The Genographic Project needs DNA samples from hundreds of thousands of people around the world to trace human ancestry and movements of people in ancient times. Dr. Spencer Wells, the project's director, is at Grand Central Station in New York City to find volunteers to provide cheek swabs or samples of their DNA for this project.

Wells finds and interviews four people (Dee Dee, Frank, Cecile, and J. W.) who agree to provide samples and to tell Wells what they know about their ancestry. The swabs are sent to a lab to be analyzed. After a few weeks, Wells meets with the four people and tells them what their DNA has revealed about their family histories. He emphasizes the point that everyone on Earth has one common place of origin—East Africa—and therefore we are all related genetically.

For a video of Dr. Wells collecting samples in Astoria, Queens (featured in Reading A) and explanations of how DNA is traced in men and women, view the video at: http://www.youtube.com/watch?v=pyOS05GUze0

Before Viewing

Exercise A. | Using a Dictionary

- Ask students to work individually to become familiar with some of the key vocabulary in the video by looking up the words in the box and completing the definitions.
- Compare answers as a class.
- Ask for volunteers to use each of the words in a new sentence.

Vocabulary Notes

The DNA samples are coded so that researchers know which people they came from, but they appear *anonymous* to the lab workers, who know nothing about the person's name or appearance. This is done so the results cannot be influenced by anything other than the genetic material.

Answer Key

1. heritage 2. separate 3. anonymously

Exercise B. | Brainstorming

After students have a chance to talk with a partner, ask pairs to tell the class their ideas.

Answer Key

Possible answers:
There are a lot of people there. The people are from many different ethnicities/races. There are people of all ages and backgrounds.

While Viewing

Exercise A.

- Ask students to read the questions in exercise **A** so they are prepared to watch and listen for certain information.
- Play the video. Ask students to circle their answers as they watch. If necessary, play the video again.
- Tell the class you will go over the answers in the next exercise.

After Viewing

Exercise A.

- Have students discuss the statements in the While Viewing section and compare answers. Remind them to correct the false statements.
- Play the video again and check answers.

Answer Key

1. F (They left about 45,000 years ago.)
2. T
3. F (Cecile's last name is Nepal, but she comes from the Philippines.)
4. T

Exercise B. | Synthesizing

- Tell students to consider information from Reading A and the video as they respond to the two questions.
- Point out the word *because* in the second sentence. Explain that it is important to support an opinion (*I think / I don't think*) with reasons.

Answer Key

Answers will vary.

Preparing to Read

(pages 50–51)

WARM-UP

The Lesson B target vocabulary is presented in two exercises: first in a paragraph where the students are able to get meaning from context; they are then asked to match the words with their definitions. The second exercise first provides definitions and then asks the students to complete a paragraph with the new words.

Exercise A. | Building Vocabulary

- Have students read the paragraph and do the matching individually.

- Check answers as a class.

- Point out the first **CT Focus** box, which gives additional practice in identifying sentences as fact or speculation. The word *probably* signals that the first given sentence is a speculation, whereas the second sentence is a factual statement about what archaeologists found.

Answer Key

1. d 2. e 3. a 4. c 5. b

Exercise B. | Building Vocabulary

- In this second section, definitions of the words as used in the main passage are provided. Students must use them appropriately to complete the paragraph.

- When students have completed the exercise individually, ask them to compare answers in pairs.

- Check answers by inviting volunteers to read out the completed sentences of the paragraph.

- Draw students' attention to the **Word Partners** box. Ask students to suggest sentences using each of these phrases. For example, *My sister and I grew up in the same house, but we have nothing in common.*

- Remind students to list word partners in their vocabulary notebooks.

Answer Key

1. common 2. alive 3. journey 4. reach
5. descendants

IDEAS FOR... Expansion

For **Word Partners,** you may want to have a timed activity where students talk with classmates to find out what they have in common. Start by having students brainstorm a list of their interests. These might include favorite music, sports, hobbies, foods, etc. Announce that students must talk with someone they usually don't partner with in class. They have one minute to compare interests to see what they have in common. Announce when the time is up and have students change partners and repeat the exercise. At the end, ask for volunteers to say what they had in common with classmates.

Exercise C. | Using Vocabulary

- Remind students to use complete sentences in their answers to the questions.

- While students share their sentences with a partner, circulate through the classroom listening unobtrusively to students' interactions. Make sure that both partners are participating equally.

Exercise D. | Thinking Ahead

- The aim of this exercise is to activate background knowledge about the topics featured in the reading passage. If students don't know the answers, ask them to guess.

- Tell students you will check the answers after the reading.

Answer Key

1. East Africa (paragraph A) 2. 60,000 (paragraph C)
3. by land (paragraph I)

Exercise E. | Predicting

- Ask students to use the pictures and subheads to predict the reading topic.

- Note: Students will check their predictions later, in exercise **A** on page 54.

track **1-08**

Ask students to read the article on pages 52 and 53.

Overview of the Reading

The reading is organized around an overview of human movements as shown on the central map. The sequence of events is numbered, with elaboration in each of the corresponding paragraphs.

There are many facets to National Geographic's Genographic Project. At http://ngm.nationalgeographic.com/ngm/0603/feature2/map.html you can see the map on which the map in the reading was based. It offers more information about key archaeological sites where human remains and artifacts were found, as well as dates for those sites. See a feature article on the human journey at http://ngm.nationalgeographic.com/2006/03/human-journey/shreeve-text

Understanding the Reading (page 54)

45 mins

Exercise A. | Understanding the Gist

Check students' predictions in exercise **E** on page 51.

Answer Key

The correct answer is b. This is an overview of the migration of our ancestors—not a focus of one person's family (a) or of one major lineage such as Native Americans (c).

Exercise B. | Identifying Sequence

- Tell students to use the numbers from the map and text to put the eight events in order. Point out that the order is from longest ago (the largest number of years) to most recent.

- Allow students time to work individually. Remind them that they should be able to say where they found the supporting information.

- Check answers as a class.

Answer Key

The correct order (with the paragraph letter where each event is described and the approximate number of years ago the event happened):

1=6. (paragraph B: 195,000)

2=3. (paragraph C: 60,000)

3=8. (paragraph D: 50,000)

4=4. (paragraph E: 45,000)

5=7. (paragraph G: 40,000)

6=2. (paragraph H: 26,000)

7=1. (paragraph I: 25,000–30,000)

8=5. (paragraph J: 13,000)

Exercise C. | Identifying Fact and Speculation

- Ask students to work in pairs to go through the text to find both kinds of examples. Suggest that they circle signal words found in speculations and underline sentences about facts.

- Check answers as a class. Ask four volunteers to read one of their sentences.

Answer Key

Most of the text consists of facts. Aside from the example given about Omo I and Omo II, most of the other speculations involve the word *probably*. Students' examples of speculations should come from points 3, 6 (×2), 7, 8. Also, the caption for the Cactus Hill photograph says *"may be* some of the oldest . . ."

> **IDEAS FOR... Expansion**
>
> Have students look at the speculations containing the word *probably* and suggest reasons why the author chose not to present the idea as a fact. For example, in point 3, about leaving Africa, perhaps there are no archaeological sites with human remains or artifacts dating from 50,000 years ago that would provide a definite idea of the route.

Exercise D. | Critical Thinking: Speculating

- Allow time for students to discuss the questions in pairs.

- Tell students that although they may have different ideas, they must be able to explain and support their opinions.

- When the pairs finish, lead a brief class discussion about the questions.

> **TIP** Make students aware that multiple answers are possible to questions such as these. Encourage the class to think creatively as well as critically.

Exercise E. | Synthesizing

- Students consider information from both readings and the video as they discuss the questions in small groups.

- One point to keep in mind is that most people have mixed backgrounds because over the years their ancestors intermarried with other ethnic groups. For example, both Pedro and Frank seem to have some Native American ancestors who migrated from Asia over the land bridge to the Americas, but in more recent centuries, their families may have intermarried with Spanish families who settled in Mexico and South America starting about 500 years ago.

Exploring Written English
(pages 55–57)

45 mins

In this lesson, students go through the process of writing sentences about three members of their family. The lesson starts with a review of the simple past and then follows the steps in the writing process. In their final sentences, students can write facts or speculations about each person.

Exercise A. | Language for Writing

- Go over the information in the box.
- Check comprehension of the grammar by asking for volunteers to give a sentence with some of the past forms given in the box.
- Have students complete the exercise individually and then compare answers in pairs.
- Check answers with the class by asking volunteers to each write an answer on the board. Encourage students to correct their spelling as necessary.

Answer Key

1. moved	**5.** were, lived
2. decided	**6.** made
3. studied, found	**7.** stopped
4. learned, came	**8.** had

Exercise B.

- Have students create their own sentences using the simple past.
- Monitor students as they work, and help them with ideas as needed.
- If possible, collect and correct students' work.

Answer Key

Answers will vary.

IDEAS FOR...   Grammar Review

The Student Handbook on page 215 provides a summary of the simple past.

Exercise C. | Speculating

- Go over the information in the Writing Skill box. Point out that common ways to express speculation are presented, along with the stylistic suggestion that students use a variety of words and phrases to avoid repetition when expressing speculation.

- Some additional words or phrases used for speculation are *perhaps*, *maybe*, and *it's likely*.
- Students work in pairs to transform the sentences from facts to speculations. Make sure students know that there are several ways to rewrite the sentences. Encourage them to use a different word or phrase in each of their sentences.
- Ask for volunteers to read aloud one or two of their sentences.

Answer Key

Possible answers:
1. I believe my friend's mother lived in England when she was a child. **2.** My great-grandparents probably came from Korea. **3.** It's possible that my ancestors were hunters. **4.** I think my grandfather has a lot of old photographs of his recent ancestors.

Exercise D. | Critical Thinking: Analyzing

- Have students complete the sentences individually and then compare answers in pairs.
- Check answers as a class by asking volunteers to read their sentences aloud.

Answer Key

Possible answers:
2. It's possible that my grandfather was a farmer.
3. My mother came to New York when she was a teenager. **4.** My mother never met her grandmother.
5. It might be true that my grandfather visited Egypt when he was young.

IDEAS FOR...   Presenting Grammar

After exercise **D,** ask students to think about situations where they are not sure about their family history and therefore must speculate. Be sure to point out that speculating often means making inferences, or educated guesses. Point out that there's nothing wrong with saying you're not sure!

Writing Task: Drafting

(page 58)

Exercise A. | Brainstorming

- Remind students that brainstorming is a useful first step for gathering ideas before writing.

- Ask students to quickly write all the names of family members they can think of. The idea here is to get students thinking about their relatives, which in turn may trigger memories or information about them in the next step.

Exercise B. | Planning

- Go over the steps in this exercise.

- Remind students that complete sentences are not necessary at this stage and that it is more important to focus on their ideas than on grammar, spelling, or punctuation.

- Encourage students to make notes about several things for each person so they can choose two to write about later.

- Walk around and monitor students' work. Provide assistance as needed.

Exercise C. | Draft 1

As students write their sentences, walk around and offer help as needed. Refrain from any type of error correction at this point.

Writing Task: Revising and Editing *(page 59)*

Exercise D. | Peer Evaluation

- Go over the steps in the evaluation process to make sure students know what to do.

- Ensure that both members of each pair have equal time to give feedback.

- Remind students that positive feedback is just as important as constructive criticism.

Exercise E. | Draft 2

- Walk around and monitor students as they work. Provide assistance as needed.

- Remind students to use the feedback they got from their partner.

Exercise F. | Editing Practice

- Go over the information in the box. Answer any questions that may arise.

- Allow time for students to read and correct the sentences.

- Check the answers by asking students to read out the corrected sentences and explain the errors.

Answer Key

1. My grandparents **were** born in Seoul, Korea.
2. My mother **studied** science when she was in college.
3. My grandmother **took** her children south after the war.
4. My aunt and uncle **came** to America last year.
5. I **discovered** a lot of interesting information about my family history.
6. I think my great-grandmother **studied** medicine and worked in a hospital.

Writing Task: Editing

(page 60)

Exercise G. | Editing Checklist

- Read the sentences in the editing checklist.
- Allow time for students to read and edit their work.
- Ask for some examples of each type of error.

Exercise H. | Final Draft

Have students complete their final draft, and then collect their work.

Unit Quiz

- Students can work in groups to answer the questions.
- Encourage students to refer back to the relevant pages of the unit to find the answers.
- To do the quiz as a competition, you can have students work in teams.

Answer Key

1. genealogy	**5.** separate
2. ancestors	**6.** probably
3. DNA	**7.** common
4. speculation	**8.** artwork

IDEAS FOR... **Expansion**

If students are interested in family history, they could create a display of their family's recent past. This might include maps, pictures of where they have lived (many are available online, so personal photographs are not necessary), and stories about memorable events. Students could take turns presenting their display to the rest of the class.

IDEAS FOR... **Further Research**

Family trees can be used for more than biological families. Music writer Pete Frame organized Rock Family Trees to show the interrelationships of rock-'n'-roll groups through the years. BBC produced a series of programs on this theme. For more information, visit http://www.bbc.co.uk/programmes/b0070y2d

The Trouble with Trash

Academic Track: Environmental Science/Sociology

Academic Pathways: Lesson A: Finding supporting ideas
Analyzing causes and effects
Lesson B: Understanding a multimodal text
Lesson C: Using details to clarify ideas
Writing sentences to make suggestions

Unit Theme

When people throw away trash, it doesn't just disappear. Environmental activists and artists work to create awareness of the problems that trash causes and to promote recycling.

Unit 4 explores the topic of trash as it relates to:

– an "island" of plastic in the Pacific Ocean
– an artist who creates trash sculptures
– another artist who makes art from a landfill
– being environmentally responsible

Think and Discuss *(page 61)*

5 mins

- Ask students to describe the picture. What is the setting for this photo? Who produced all this trash? (Answer: The trash was left by climbers on Mount Everest. A local guide called a sherpa is sorting the trash.) Ask students what kinds of things mountain climbers might throw away. Why did they leave them there? (In the photo, you can see plastics, a metal ladder, bags of trash, and yellow nylon tents. Climbers used them to climb the mountain but didn't take the objects away with them.) Ask how people get to Mount Everest and how the trash will be taken away. (Answer: Typically, people fly to high-altitude base camps in small planes. It will be expensive to remove the trash that way, and it cannot be recycled nearby.)

- Discuss question 1 as a class. Start by brainstorming different words for *trash* such as *garbage* and *solid waste*. What are some of the major categories of garbage? Which ones can be used again and in what form? (Answers: Metals such as steel and aluminum, paper, plastics, glass—all can be recycled. Also, auto batteries and tires can be recycled.)

- Discuss question 2. (Possible answer: Some biodegradable materials decompose or fall apart, but plastic and metals last for a very long time. Garbage takes up a lot of space.)

Exploring the Theme

15 mins

(pages 62–63)

The opening spread features a photograph of the trash produced by an average U.S. family in one year.

- Ask students to read the caption at the bottom of page 62 and examine the photo. What kinds of things do students throw away every day? How many of them could be *recycled* or used again? Is recycling made easy where they live or study? Are there any incentives to recycle? For example, in some places, you get money back when you recycle glass bottles and aluminum cans.

- Ask students to answer the questions in B. In the paragraph about Cheung Yan, it should be clear that the paper gets recycled several times. In the other paragraph, note that it is common in some urban neighborhoods in the U.S. for people to put unwanted items on the sidewalk, hoping someone will take them away. If people disposed of their unwanted things properly, they would have to pay a fee to have them taken away.

Answer Key

B. 1. Paper **2.** She sold furniture and electronics that people threw away.

> **TIP** Ask how trash is collected where students live. Do they have to take trash somewhere or pay for someone to take it away? Do they have to sort it first?

IDEAS FOR... Expansion

Ask students what they do with old cell phones, computers, and other electronics. Have students research *electronic trash* or *e-waste* online. Alternatively, ask them to read about the topic at http://ngm.nationalgeographic.com/2008/01/high-tech-trash/carroll-text

30 mins

Preparing to Read *(page 64)*

WARM-UP

The Lesson A target vocabulary is presented through an exercise that asks students to use context to complete sentences by choosing between two words.

Ask what happens to trash after it is collected. (Answer: Some is burned and buried in landfills, and other trash—including medical waste and toxic materials—is sometimes dumped at sea.)

Exercise A. | Building Vocabulary

- Have students find the words in the reading and use the other words around them to guess their meanings. Then have them complete the sentences using one of the two words or phrases.

- Check the answers by asking volunteers to read out a sentence each.

- Point out the **Word Partners** box. Remind students that these word partners are sometimes called collocations.

> **TIP** Review some of the clues that context words provide to identify the part of speech of target vocabulary items. Most of the target vocabulary items in this lesson are verbs. In the reading passage, some of these appear as gerunds that are the subject of sentences. For example, in paragraph I, *cleaning up* is the subject of the first sentence and *making people aware* is the subject of the second sentence.

Answer Key

1. clean up	**6.** recycle
2. notice	**7.** take action
3. collect	**8.** throw away
4. cause	**9.** report
5. solution	**10.** be aware of

Exercise B. | Using Vocabulary

- Allow time for students to work in pairs to discuss the questions.
- Invite volunteers to share their answers with the class.

Exercise C. | Brainstorming

- Give students a minute or two to write down everything they can think of that's made of plastic. After students compare answers in pairs, open up the discussion to the whole class.

- Make a list on the board, asking students to contribute items that are not already on the list.

Answer Key

Possible answers:
bottles, bags, garden hoses, light switches, wastebaskets, CD and DVD boxes

Exercise D. | Predicting

- Remind the class that predicting is trying to guess the gist, or general idea, of the reading passage. Point out how the question is phrased as "What do you think the reading is mainly about?" It is important for taking exams that students realize that questions about the gist or main idea can be phrased in different ways.

- Ask students to use the title, pictures, and captions to predict what the reading is about. Write their predictions on the board.

- Note: Students will check their prediction later, in exercise **A** on page 67.

 track 1-09 Ask students to read the passage. Explain that the vocabulary definitions in the footnotes at the bottom of page 66 will help them understand the reading.

> ### IDEAS FOR... Expansion
>
> Ask students to search Google for images of the Great Pacific Garbage Patch. Some images show the plastic, while others have maps that show the extent of the plastic "island" and its location. Still other maps show how the currents work to create a vortex, or whirling spiral motion, that pulls things like plastic trash into it.

Overview of the Reading

The passage describes a huge mass of plastic debris floating in the North Pacific Ocean. Discarded plastic from Asia and North America has become trapped in spinning ocean currents, ever growing into a larger mass. Although some of the trash is identifiable bottles and bags, much of it consists of tiny pieces of plastic. The garbage kills animals that eat it and blocks sunlight from deeper water; this in turn kills plankton and algae, the food source for many fish. The passage also discusses how environmentalists are trying to raise awareness of the problem and seek solutions.

To learn more about the huge garbage patch and the problems it presents, visit the site at **http://education. nationalgeographic.com/education/encyclopedia/ great-pacific-garbage-patch/kd/?ar_a=3&ar_r=3**

IDEAS FOR... Checking Comprehension

Ask these questions or write them on the board.

1. What is an ocean current? (a regular and predictable strong movement of the sea) If you have Internet access in the classroom, a short video explains ocean currents at http://www.natgeoeducationvideo.com/film/1051/ocean-currents

2. Why doesn't the plastic just disappear? (Plastic is not biodegradable; it will not break down. Plastics can last for hundreds of years.)

3. What are two reasons you can't see the plastic island from the air? (It is mostly tiny pieces of plastic that don't show up, and much of the plastic is below the surface.)

4. What does Harada mean when he says everyone can take action? (Individuals—not just NGOs or governments—can do something about environmental problems.)

Understanding the Reading *(page 67)*

Exercise A. | Understanding the Gist

Check students' prediction(s) in exercise **D** on page 64. Did they guess the general idea correctly?

Answer Key

The correct answer is item c. Item a is too general: This passage focuses on one particular area of pollution and its causes. Item b is wrong because the area of garbage is in the Pacific Ocean, not on land.

Exercise B. | Getting the Main Idea

The second half of item a is not true; scientists know the source of the plastics because of the ocean currents. Item c is a supporting detail—not the main idea. If students' prediction was correct in exercise **A**, they should have chosen item b as the main idea of the passage.

Exercise C. | Identifying Key Details

- Remind students that a statement must be completely true to be marked that way. False statements can be corrected with information from the passage so that they are true. Although students are not directed to correct the false statements, encourage them to get in the habit of doing so.

- Allow time for students to go back to the reading and mark their answers.

- Check the answers as a class.

Answer Key

1. T
2. F (a racing boat captain, not a scientist)
3. F (six years, not one year)
4. T
5. F (small pieces, not large)
6. T
7. F (teaching people around the world about ocean garbage)
8. T

Exercise D. | Critical Thinking: Analyzing Causes and Effects

- Ask students to work in pairs to find and underline the information in the reading that describes the causes of garbage islands. Most of this information is in paragraphs B and D.

- Draw students' attention to the **CT Focus** box. Make sure students understand that *causes* are reasons for something happening and *effects* are the results.

- Remind the class that a graphic organizer is a visual way to show the relationship between ideas in a reading. The arrow shows that the reasons in the left box bring about the results in the right box.

- Check the answers as a class.

Answer Key

Causes:
- plastic objects like bottles and bags
- spin around in a giant circle

Effects:
- eat
- surface, sunlight

Exercise E. | Critical Thinking: Analyzing Problems and Solutions

- Have students work in pairs to identify and underline solutions to the problem described in the reading.

- Lead a class discussion about things that people can do to help clean up the ocean.

Answer Key

But making people aware of the problem will help.
Another idea is to recycle the plastic garbage.
Other: People can use and throw away plastic more responsibly. They could also use less plastic by using reusable bags and bottles.

IDEAS FOR... **Expansion**

In an increasing number of countries, single-use plastic shopping bags are banned or people have to pay for them. Shoppers are encouraged to bring their own reusable cloth or plastic bags. Do students think people will act more responsibly if they are forced to think about how they will carry groceries and other purchases?

Developing Reading Skills *(page 68)*

45 mins

Reading Skill: Finding Supporting Ideas

track **1-10**

- Go over the information in the box. It shows how supporting ideas give *reasons*—the "why"—or *examples*—telling "what" or "how"—to make the main idea stronger.

- It is helpful if students keep these points in mind as they read and also when they write. Encourage them to notice words such as *because, reason, for instance,* and *for example,* which often signal supporting ideas.

Exercise A. | Matching

- Allow students time to decide which supporting ideas from the right column give extra information about the main ideas in the left column.

- Check answers with the class.

Answer Key

1. c (why) **2.** a (how) **3.** b (what)

Exercise B. | Finding Supporting Ideas

- Ask students to return to the reading passage to find supporting ideas in order to answer the questions.

- Invite volunteers to read their answers aloud.

Answer Key

1. The currents draw in new plastic objects and keep the existing ones from escaping.
2. Sea turtles think the plastic bags are jellyfish and eat them. Seabirds eat the plastic rings from six packs. Also, the microplastics near the surface block sunlight, and the lack of sunlight kills very small sea creatures like plankton and algae, leaving less food for the larger fish.
3. He made the boat from plastic bottles to teach people about the problem of ocean garbage.

Viewing: Trash People
(page 69)

Overview of the Video

German artist H. A. Schult used trash found in a landfill to create 1,000 sculptures of people. He displays his sculptures in many countries to make the point that garbage is a global problem. Schult believes that the children of today realize that everything on Earth is interconnected. He thinks they will find a solution to the garbage problem.

Search online using the keywords *Schult trash people images*. Some images show hundreds of them assembled at well-known sites such as the pyramids at Giza.

Before Viewing

Exercise A. | Using a Dictionary

- Students become familiar with some of the key vocabulary in the video by looking up the words in the box and using them to complete sentences.
- Compare answers as a class.
- Ask for volunteers to use each of the words in a new sentence.
- Note that some of this vocabulary will be recycled in Reading B.

Vocabulary Notes

Some art—like paintings and drawings—is flat or two-dimensional. Sculpture is three-dimensional art made from solid materials such as stone, metal, or other hard substances. Schult worked with trash to *transform,* or radically change, it from useless garbage to art. Ask the class about sculptures they know, either in their communities or famous examples such as Rodin's *The Thinker.*

Answer Key

1. sculpt 2. Garbage collectors 3. transform
4. landfill

Exercise B. | Brainstorming

After students have a chance to talk with a partner, ask pairs to tell the class about what artists could do with trash. Return to this question after students read the passage.

While Viewing

Exercise A.

- Ask students to read the questions silently.
- Tell students to keep the questions in mind as they watch the video.
- Play the video again and have students answer the questions.

Answer Key

1. b
2. a
3. a, b, c, d, f, g (France is not mentioned, and South Africa is discussed in the context of receiving garbage from other places.)

After Viewing

Exercise A.

- Have students discuss answers.
- When students give their answers to question 3, ask them to support the countries they name with details about the locations. In the script, each country is associated with a famous or iconic place such as the Great Wall in China or the Matterhorn in Switzerland.
- If necessary, play the video again to check answers.

Exercise B. | Synthesizing/Evaluating

After considering each person's point of view, students give and support an opinion about whose perspective is best.

Answer Key

Both Rothschild and Schult aim to create awareness of trash issues, but Harada encourages people to take action.

Preparing to Read

30 mins

(pages 70–71)

WARM-UP

Part of Lesson B's target vocabulary is first introduced before students actively use the words in an exercise. The rest of the items are presented in a matching exercise.

Exercise A. | Building Vocabulary

- Ask students to choose if they want to work individually or in pairs.

- Explain that the words in blue are the new vocabulary words given with definitions. The task is to use the words appropriately to complete the sentences.

- Have students compare answers in pairs before checking answers as a class.

Answer Key

1. combine 2. company 3. create 4. deal with
5. material

Exercise B. | Building Vocabulary

- In this second exercise, students must infer the meaning of the target vocabulary item from context and then match the sentence parts to make definitions.

- Draw students' attention to the **Word Partners** box describing how the preposition *despite* introduces a phrase that is opposed or contrasted later in the sentence. *Despite* has the same meaning as *even though* or *in spite of*.

- Have the class practice using *despite* with the following sentence starters:
  Despite the bad weather, . . .
  Despite not feeling hungry, . . .
  Despite the heavy traffic, . . .
  Listen for statements opposite in meaning to the *despite* phrase.

Answer Key

1. b 2. d 3. a 4. e 5. c

Exercise C. | Using Vocabulary

- Remind students to respond to the questions with complete sentences.

- While students share their sentences in pairs, circulate through the classroom listening unobtrusively to students' interactions. Make sure that both partners are participating equally.

Answer Key

For item 2, the answers are red and yellow for orange, and red and blue for purple.

Exercise D. | Predicting

- The aim of this exercise is to have students use information from an image to predict the content of a reading passage. The site is a landfill, and the people working on it are garbage collectors. Closer examination shows that the workers—most of whom are wearing bright green vests—are holding large plastic bags and seem to be collecting something. Students might think that Vik Muniz is the workers' supervisor or boss, but he isn't.

- Note: Students will check their predictions later, after they read the passage.

Answer Key

Answers will vary. (See above.)

track **1-11** Ask students to read the article.

Overview of the Reading

The article describes how artist Vik Muniz worked with garbage pickers at a landfill in Brazil to create huge photographs of workers and garbage. The images sold for high prices, and Muniz gave the money to the workers' organization. In addition, the project raised the self-esteem of the workers.

The general theme of the lesson is recycling: using discarded materials in new ways. The garbage pickers search for materials such as aluminum cans and glass bottles that they sell to recycling companies. The graph and its caption discuss what kinds of materials Americans recycle compared to what they burn or put in landfills. Artist Muniz—like Schult in the video—recycles trash as art.

National Geographic's Green Living website http://greenliving.nationalgeographic.com/reduce-reuse-recycle/ promotes the three-part strategy of *reduce*, *reuse*, and *recycle*. People can reduce waste by buying things with less packaging. They can reuse things like plastic bottles and glass jars, or by buying things at second-hand shops. If they must throw things out, they should try to do so responsibly by putting them where they will be recycled.

Understanding the Reading *(page 74)*

Exercise A. | Understanding the Gist

Check students' predictions in exercise **D** on page 71.

Answer Key

1. The people are at a landfill. It's a dirty and dangerous place.
2. The man is an artist.
3. The people behind him are garbage collectors. They're hunting through the garbage for recyclable cans, bottles, and other materials.

Exercise B. | Scanning for Key Details

- Remind students that key details give reasons, examples, or more information about main ideas in a reading.
- Students use words from the text and indicate the paragraph where they were found.
- Check answers as a class.

Answer Key

1. landfills (A) 2. color, depth (C) 3. $20, $25 (B)
4. workers' organization (D)

Exercise C. | Identifying Supporting Ideas

- Have students complete the task individually and then compare answers in pairs.
- Check answers as a class.

Answer Key

1. hunt for recyclable materials, sell objects to recycling companies 2. He explains the importance of recycling.
3. Muniz gave money from the pictures to the workers' organization. Because other people valued the pictures, the workers started to see themselves differently.

Exercise D. | Critical Thinking: Analyzing Graphs

- Spend a few minutes reviewing how graphs work. The one on page 73 is a bar graph where the labeled categories of trash are given along the horizontal axis and quantities are shown on the vertical axis in millions of tons. The horizontal line indicates that things above it are recycled while things below it are incinerated or buried in a landfill.

- After everyone has had a chance to complete the exercise, check answers as a class, asking students to support their answers with reference to the graph.

Answer Key

Mostly recycled: paper, yard trimmings
Mostly incinerated or landfilled: food scraps, plastics, glass

Exercise E. | Critical Thinking: Synthesizing

Schult and Muniz use art, whereas all three use trash to make people aware of the problems.

Answer Key

S, M
R, S, M
R, S, M

TIP	If you don't have time to replay the video, suggest that students use the video script on page 205 for review.

Exploring Written English

(pages 75–76)

45 mins

In this lesson, students go through the process of writing sentences about what people should do to be more environmentally responsible. The lesson starts with a review of language for giving advice and making suggestions.

Exercise A. | Language for Writing

- Go over the information in the box. Make sure students understand the difference between advice and suggestions.

- Allow students time to unscramble the sentences individually and then compare answers in pairs.

- Check the answers as a class by inviting volunteers to write the unscrambled sentences on the board.

Answer Key

1. The school could start a recycling program.
2. The school should use solar energy.
3. We ought to repair broken things.
4. Stores shouldn't use plastic bags.
5. People ought to turn down the heat.

Exercise B.

- Explain the task. Students are to use the cues in parentheses to write sentences with *could* or *should*.

- Have students work individually to write their sentences.

- Check answers as a class by asking volunteers to read out their sentences. Write the correct answers on the board.

Answer Key

1. We could make people aware of the problem of garbage islands.
2. We should not waste food
3. People could buy fewer things.
4. People should not buy water in plastic bottles.
5. Students should/ought to use recycled paper in school.
6. Art students could make art objects from trash at school.

> **IDEAS FOR... Grammar Review**
>
> The Student Handbook on page 216 provides an overview of giving advice and making suggestions. Giving advice is considered stronger than making suggestions. Ask the class about situations where it would be more appropriate to make suggestions than give advice. For example, if students are meeting with environmental experts, it would be rude to give them advice!

Exercise C.

- Have students work in small groups to think of environmental problems at their school or in their city/town and suggest solutions.

- Walk around as students talk, offering help or suggestions as needed.

Writing Skill: Using Details to Clarify Ideas

Go over the information in the box. Point out the use of *such as* to introduce examples.

Exercise D. | Identifying Details

- Allow time for students to read the sentences and identify those that contain examples.

- Ask volunteers to read the sentences aloud and write the detail words on the board.

Answer Key

3. such as clothes and toys 4. for example, newspapers, glass, and plastic 6. such as garbage islands

Exercise E. | Matching

- Students match ideas with details and rewrite the sentences to reflect them.

- After students complete the matching task, check the answers as a class.

Answer Key

1. We should recycle bottles, such as plastic water bottles. 2. Garbage islands are a problem for wildlife, such as sea turtles and birds. 3. We should try to recycle more of our waste, such as paper, plastic, and glass.

Writing Task: Drafting
(page 78)

Exercise A. | Brainstorming

- Ask students to work in pairs to quickly write down all the things that people could do to be more environmentally responsible. Encourage them to use ideas from the unit or their own ideas.

- Lead a brief class discussion to share ideas for how to be environmentally responsible.

Exercise B. | Planning

- Go over the steps in this exercise.

- Remind students that complete sentences are not necessary at this stage and that it is more important to focus on their ideas than on grammar or spelling.

- As students work individually, walk around and monitor their work. Provide assistance as needed.

Exercise C. | Draft 1

As students write their sentences, walk around and offer help if asked. Refrain from any type of error correction at this point, but provide assistance as needed.

Writing Task: Revising and Editing *(page 79)*

Exercise D. | Peer Evaluation

- Go over the steps in the evaluation process to make sure students know what to do.

- Have students use the three steps to help them read their partner's work. Point out the importance of making sure advice or suggestions relate to the main idea and that the sentences provide details.

- Make sure that both members of the pair have equal time to give feedback.

Exercise E. | Draft 2

- Walk around and monitor students as they work. Provide assistance as needed.

- Remind students to use the feedback they got from their partner when writing their second draft.

Exercise F. | Editing Practice

- Go over the information in the box.

- Allow time for students to find and correct the errors in the sentences.

- Go over the sentences as a class, asking students to read out the correct sentences and explain the errors.

Answer Key

1. People could to recycle computer paper by printing on both sides.
2. The school ought **to** turn off the lights at night.
3. We shouldn't **take** long showers.
4. We should to use public transportation and not drive to work.
5. We ought **to** buy less and recycle more.
6. Students could plant more trees at their school.
7. We could **save** energy if we unplug our computers at night.
8. People should **be** more aware of the environment.

Writing Task: Editing

(page 80)

Exercise G. | Editing Checklist

• Go over the sentences in the editing checklist.

• Allow time for students to read and edit their work.

Exercise H. | Final Draft

Have students complete their final draft, and then collect their work.

TIP You can use students' sentences to collect (anonymous) examples of good sentences and common errors for the next class.

Unit Quiz

• Students can work in groups to answer the questions.

• Encourage students to refer back to the relevant pages of the unit to find the answers.

• To do the quiz as a competition, you can have students work in teams.

Answer Key

1. buying, boxes
2. recycle
3. throw, away
4. Pacific Ocean
5. supporting idea
6. sculptures
7. contrasting
8. landfill

IDEAS FOR... **Grammar Review**

If students have identified ways to make people more environmentally responsible in their school, have them make signs with advice or suggestions for improvement and post them in appropriate places.

IDEAS FOR... **Further Research**

It's not only the oceans that people have polluted with garbage; trash in space is becoming a big problem. Both NASA and the European Space Agency are concerned about the accumulation of debris in space and are trying to deal with it. For more information, go to http://www.orbitaldebris. jsc.nasa.gov/ or http://www.esa.int/esaMI/ Space_Debris/SEMCIL05VQF_0.html

The World in Our Kitchen

Academic Track: Interdisciplinary

Academic Pathways   Lesson A: Scanning for key details
                                     Reflecting critically
                              Lesson B: Identifying pros and cons in a passage
                              Lesson C: Using synonyms to avoid repetition
                                       Writing sentences to express an opinion

Unit Theme

The food we eat and the equipment we use for cooking come from all over the world. Few countries are self-sufficient. Most nations import and export foods and raw materials.

Unit 5 explores the topic of food as it relates to:

– basic foods and global trade
– a man who built a toaster from scratch
– teaching sustainable agriculture
– the locavore movement

Think and Discuss *(page 81)*

- Ask students to look at the picture. Were the tomatoes produced nearby or far away? In what kind of place will they be sold? (Possible answer: Since the tomatoes are not wrapped for shipping, they probably were grown nearby and will be sold in a nearby market.)

- Discuss question 1 as a class. Brainstorm the kinds of fruits and vegetables students buy and eat. Make a list on the board. Where do students buy their fruits and vegetables? (Possible answers: grocery stores, supermarkets, farmers' markets, street vendors) Does anyone grow their own fruits and vegetables?

- Ask students if they look at the labels on fruits and vegetables to see where they were grown.

- Have students discuss question 2 in groups.

- Ask volunteers to tell the class about anything interesting that they found out from classmates.

Exploring the Theme

(pages 82–83)

The opening spread features a graph showing information about importers and exporters of grains, a map illustrating patterns of global trade, and a text about producers of iron and copper.

- The first question uses the graph and the photograph under it. Make sure students understand the words *importers* (countries that buy products from other countries) and *exporters* (countries that sell products to other countries).

- Take time to go over the concept of *grains*, a staple of many diets around the world. Wheat and corn are common in American diets, while rice is the basic grain in much of the rest of the world. Ask what grain is the most important in students' diet.

- Ask if anyone knows what the Chinese farmers in the photo are doing. (Answer: They are *winnowing*, throwing millet into the air so the inedible parts will blow away.)

- For question 2, ask students to work in pairs to identify the trade patterns on the map.

- Discuss question 3 as a class.

Answer Key

1. Japan and South Korea import a lot of grains because they lack the land to grow much of it themselves.
2. The map shows how food products move around the world each year. (Answers will vary for the second part of the item.)
3. China, Japan, Russia, and India produce a lot of iron, while most copper comes from Chile, Peru, and the United States. Some items that use iron are tools and cars; copper is used to make wire, cable, electric motors, jewelry, and bathroom fixtures, for example.

TIP   Have students look around the classroom for items made from iron or copper. Many wires are copper, but they may not be visible.

IDEAS FOR...   Expansion

Ask students to keep a food diary for three days, writing what they eat and—wherever possible—where the food came from.

Preparing to Read (page 84)

30 mins

WARM-UP

The Lesson A target vocabulary is presented in two exercises: a matching task and a sentence-completion activity.

- Check that all students know that a *toaster* is a small electrical appliance used to brown and warm bread.

Exercise A. | Building Vocabulary

- Have students find the blue words in the reading and use the other words around them to guess their meanings. Then have students work individually to match the sentence parts to form definitions.
- Check the answers by asking volunteers to read out a sentence each.
- Point out the **Word Partners** box. Ask students to suggest sentences with each of the phrases. Remind them to add the phrases with *basic* to their vocabulary notebooks.

Answer Key

1. b 2. e 3. d 4. a 5. c

Exercise B. | Building Vocabulary

- After students locate the words in the passage and guess their meanings from context, have them work individually to complete sentences with them.
- Ask students to compare answers in pairs. Then check the answers as a class.

Answer Key

1. instructions 2. task 3. consider 4. honest
5. appreciate

Exercise C. | Using Vocabulary

- Explain that students are going to apply the new vocabulary items by giving examples.
- After students work in pairs to answer the questions, open the discussion to the whole class and ask for ideas.

Answer Key

Possible answers:
1. Basic needs include food, water, and shelter.
2. We read instructions for assembling things or using software or machinery for the first time.
3. I appreciate my friends, my family, good food, nature, good books.

TIP Almost everyone has a story about when they didn't follow instructions or the instructions were poorly written. Ask for volunteers to tell their stories about what went wrong.

Exercise D. | Brainstorming

- Have students work in pairs to discuss the questions.
- Move around the room and make sure all students are participating.

Answer Key

Possible answers:
1. Refrigerator, microwave oven, radio, television, computer, coffee maker, toaster, lamps
2. The items are probably made of different materials including steel, copper, glass, and plastic.

Exercise E. | Predicting

- Students work in pairs to come up with a list of materials or parts needed to build a toaster from scratch.
- Note: Students will check their predictions later, in exercise **A** on page 87.

track 1-12

Ask students to read the passage. Remind students that the footnotes at the bottom of pages 85 and 86 will help them understand the reading.

Overview of the Reading

The passage describes the attempt by a young designer to create an electric toaster using raw materials. First, Thomas Thwaites bought and took apart a cheap toaster to understand how it worked and identify the parts. His next task was to make the basic materials. Some of these—like steel—were made from even more basic materials such as iron. Ultimately, Thwaites' toaster worked briefly, but the lesson learned was that global society is so interconnected that we need materials and expertise from all over the world to produce a simple appliance.

IDEAS FOR... Expansion

After working through the reading and answering the comprehension questions, students may be interested in watching a video of Thomas Thwaites describing his project. The video includes pictures of him going into the iron mine and several of the steps he followed in making the materials. The TED talk is at http://www.ted.com/talks/thomas_thwaites_how_i_built_a_toaster_from_scratch.html

1. Paragraph A in the reading passage describes a character in a novel. Ask about the function of this paragraph. Why did the writer include it? (Answer: The fictional character inspired Thwaites' project. In the book, it sounds as though building a toaster ought to be simple, especially for a person from a technological society. The book's author, Adams, makes the point that one individual cannot recreate technology because technology is the end result of the work of many people over many years. By the end of the toaster project, Thwaites came to agree.)

2. In paragraph G, Thwaites says, "I considered it a partial success, to be honest." What does he mean by this? What about it was successful? (Answer: The toaster worked briefly, and Thwaites learned a lot.) What about it was a failure? (Answer: The task was much more complicated than he thought it would be.)

Understanding the Reading *(page 87)*

Exercise A. | Understanding the Gist

Check students' predictions in exercise **E** on page 84. Was anyone able to come up with a complete list?

Answer Key

He needed iron to make steel, a microwave, copper, and plastic.

Exercise B. | Identifying Main Ideas

- Suggest that students read each paragraph and then look up from the text and think of what the main idea was. Once they have identified it in their own thoughts, they can find an idea in the list that is similar.

- Once students have completed the activity individually, have them compare answers in pairs.

- Discuss the answers as a class.

Answer Key

1. C **2.** H **3.** F **4.** B **5.** G

Exercise C. | Identifying Key Details

- Ask students to use information from the text to complete the sentences. Remind them that scanning is reading quickly to find specific information.

- Have students compare answers in pairs before checking them as a class.

Answer Key

b. more than a day and a half (not including the day to get iron) **c.** book **d.** about five **e.** 2010 **f.** casing and cord **g.** wires, pins for the plug **h.** store **i.** made of

Exercise D. | Sequencing

- Draw students' attention to the Strategy box. Go over the information and ask students to look for and underline the sequencing words in the passage.

- Explain the task, pointing out that some paragraphs—like B—contain several steps.

- Have students identify the sequence individually and then compare answers in pairs.

- Check answers as a class by writing the correct sequence on the board.

Answer Key

The order of the steps from top to bottom: 5, 6, 1, 9, 2, 8, 7, 3, 4.

Exercise E. | Critical Thinking: Reflecting

- Have students read the **CT Focus** box, noting that when you *reflect*, you look back on something, think carefully about it, and consider how you reacted to it.

- In this exercise, students have an opportunity to think about items that they probably take for granted. They are asked to consider why the items are useful, what they are made of, and where they are from.

- Have students work in pairs to discuss the questions.

- Lead a class discussion about household items that students use most often.

Answer Key

Answers will vary.

Developing Reading Skills *(page 88)*

45 mins

Reading Skill: Scanning for Key Details

Go over the information in the box.

Exercise A. | Scanning for Key Details

track 1-13

- To encourage students to read quickly, searching only for relevant information, consider making the task a timed activity. Allow two minutes for students to find the information and complete the chart.

- Have students compare answers in pairs.

- Check answers as a class.

Answer Key

Mali: $616, $1.69; **Japan:** $15,342, $42.03; **United States:** $29,000, $79.45

Exercise B. | Scanning for Key Details

- Have students work individually to complete the concept map.

- Monitor students as they are working, offering assistance as needed.

- Draw the map on the board and ask volunteers to come up and write the answers in each section. Ask the rest of the class if they agree.

Answer Key

copper: mine, Wales, plug, wire
plastic: waste, melted, casing
steel: mine, England, fire, a leaf blower, microwave

IDEAS FOR...   **Visual Literacy**

Have students compare the pictures of tools on page 85, toaster parts on page 86, and Thwaites' finished toaster on page 88. What appears in all three photos? (Answer: the casing and wire cords)

Viewing: Earth University *(page 89)*

Overview of the Video

Earth University in Costa Rica prepares students to work in agriculture to promote sustainable development in Latin America, Africa, and other parts of the world. The educational emphasis is on developing practical skills by applying what students learn in the classroom to what they do in the farms and fields that form a laboratory for the university. Students learn about ecology, business management, and leadership as well as technical and scientific aspects of agriculture. In addition, students study English so they can communicate globally and keep up with developments in their field.

To learn more about this unique institution, visit the website at http://www.earth.ac.cr/?lang=en Students may find it interesting to compare how their counterparts at Earth University study with their own academic program. Details are available under the tab "Study at Earth" on the home page.

In 2008, two Earth University graduates were selected as part of National Geographic's Emerging Explorers program. Read about them and the university at http://news.nationalgeographic.com/news/2008/04/080422-earth-university.html

Before Viewing

Exercise A. | Using a Dictionary

- Students become familiar with some of the key vocabulary in the video by looking up the words in the box and completing the definitions.
- Have students work individually and then compare answers in pairs.
- Check the answers as a class.
- Ask for volunteers to use each of the words in a new sentence.

Vocabulary Note

Economic development often occurs at the expense of destroying the natural environment. For example, in the Amazon rain forest, trees have been cut down and roads built to support farming, but irreplaceable resources have been lost. By contrast, *sustainable* development seeks to retain a balance between economic growth and protecting natural resources.

Answer Key

1. Ecology 2. sustainable 3. Profit 4. community
5. Methods

Exercise B. | Predicting

- Have students work in pairs to predict what the video will be about on the basis of the title, the photo, and the words in exercise **A**.
- After students view the video, check the answer as a class.

Answer Key

c

While Viewing

Exercise A.

- Have students read the items silently before you play the video.
- After students have watched the video, have them complete the matching task individually.
- Tell the class you will check answers during the next activity.

Answer Key

1. a 2. c 3. d 4. f 5. b 6. e

After Viewing

Exercise A.

- Have students discuss and compare answers to the matching exercise.
- Play the video again. If necessary, refer students to the video script on pages 205–206.

Exercise B. | Personalizing

- Allow time for students to work in pairs to discuss their answers to the preceding exercise.
- Lead a brief class discussion about the personalized questions.

> **TIP** Encourage students to visit Earth University's website before they respond to the second question.

Answer Key

Answers will vary.

Preparing to Read

30 mins

(pages 90–91)

WARM-UP

The Lesson B target vocabulary is presented in an exercise where students are asked to use context to identify meanings.

Exercise A. | Building Vocabulary

- Have students complete the task individually and then compare answers in pairs.

- After checking answers, draw students' attention to the **Word Partners** box. Remind students that using collocations like these can help to make their writing sound more confident and fluent.

Answer Key

1. a 2. b 3. a 4. b 5. a 6. a 7. a 8. b 9. b 10. a

Exercise B. | Using Vocabulary

- Remind students to respond to the questions with complete sentences.

- While students share their sentences with a partner, circulate through the classroom listening unobtrusively to students' interactions. Make sure that both partners are participating equally.

Answer Key

Answers will vary.

IDEAS FOR... Expansion

For **Word Partners**, ask students to bring in photographs of current fashion trends as worn by celebrities. Many websites and magazines specialize in showing famous people wearing the latest trends in clothing. Sharing photos with the class provides a natural opportunity to introduce a new compound word: *trendsetter*, someone who establishes a new fashion or way of doing things that other people imitate.

Exercise C. | Scanning/Predicting

- Allow time for students to scan the passage and choose the main idea.

- Note: Students will check their predictions later, after they read the passage.

track 1-14

Ask students to read the article. Point out that the footnotes at the bottom of pages 92 and 93 will help them understand the reading.

Overview of the Reading

The reading passage is about the locavore movement, the idea that it is better to eat food from small, local farms rather from large, multinational corporate farms. Supporters believe that eating locally produced food is better for the environment because of lower transportation and packaging costs. Locavores also think local food is healthier because it's fresher and has fewer preservatives.

Critics of the locavore movement disagree with these points, saying that it depends on the type of food that is produced, the climates where people live, and the overall costs to the consumer.

Understanding the Reading *(page 94)*

Exercise A. | Understanding the Gist

Check students' predictions in exercise **C** on page 91.

Answer Key

The correct answer is a. The article presents arguments for and against the consumption of locally grown food. Corporate farms are mentioned as a detail, but their actions are not the main idea of the passage. Option c is incorrect because no specific types of foods are given in the health argument.

Exercise B. | Identifying Main Ideas

- Students decide whether the sentences represent the main idea of a paragraph or are a detail.

- Allow students time to work individually. Remind the class that skimming is a useful strategy to find the gist of a text. In this case, they should skim a paragraph, think of what the main idea is, and then compare that with the sentence for that paragraph.

- Check answers as a class.

Answer Key

1. M 2. D 3. D 4. M 5. M

Exercise C. | Classifying

- Explain to students that when you classify, you put ideas into categories. In this case, the two categories are advantages and disadvantages of being a locavore.

- Give students a few minutes to individually identify advantages and disadvantages. Then have them compare points with a partner.

- Check the answers as a class by asking for volunteers to write the information on the board.

Answer Key

Advantages: Local food requires less packaging and transportation, both of which benefit the environment. In addition, it is healthier with fewer fertilizers, pesticides, and preservatives as well as tastier because it is fresher.
Disadvantages: Buying locally produced food may not have a big impact on the environment, especially for raising beef. Not all places can produce food year-round and locally raised food—especially organic food—may be more expensive.

IDEAS FOR... Expansion

Students might enjoy learning more about whether becoming a locavore would work for them. People in the locavore movement suggest making changes in small ways such as going to farmers' markets and choosing just five foods that you regularly eat that are available from local producers. These might include such ordinary foods as eggs, cheese, and salad greens. For suggestions on getting involved with buying local foods, visit http://www.pbs.org/now/shows/344/locavore.html

---

Exercise D. | Critical Thinking: Evaluating

- Have students work in pairs to discuss the questions.

- When students have finished answering the questions, lead a class discussion on the three issues in the exercise.

Answer Key

Possible answers:
1. Just in terms of space allocated to the arguments, the writer devotes more attention to arguments for the locavore movement than against it.
2. The response depends on whether the arguments benefit the individual, the community, or Earth's environment as a whole.
3. Possible advantages include supporting local farms which might otherwise go out of business and allowing more diversification of crops that would not be feasible to grow on a large scale. A disadvantage is that people in some areas—for example, the U.S. Midwest—have no local access to seafood. Also, being a locavore is not financially feasible for many people with low incomes.

Exercise E. | Critical Thinking: Reflecting

- Ask students to think about their own answers to the questions.

- Lead a class discussion about how students view the foods in their diet. How many students think about where foods come from, how they are grown, how they are packaged, and how long they were in transit?

Exercise F. | Synthesizing

Make sure students understand that they should revisit the map showing global trade patterns on page 83 as they discuss the reading passage in small groups. To what extent does the food they eat connect them closely to other parts of the world? Do people who produce the food get much of the price consumers pay for it? For example, the Fair Trade movement tries to ensure that farmers share in the high prices consumers are charged for coffee and chocolate.

Exploring Written English (pages 95–97)

45 mins

In this lesson, students go through the process of writing sentences about their opinions on buying local food. The lesson starts with a review of the comparative forms of adjectives and nouns, and then follows the steps in the writing process. Students create a list of pros and cons before settling on an opinion. In the final sentences, the students support their opinions with details.

Exercise A. | Language for Writing

- Go over the information in the box.
- Have students complete the chart individually and then compare answers in pairs.
- Check the comparative forms in the chart by asking volunteers to write the answers on the board.

Answer Key

1. hungrier 2. worse 3. larger 4. cheaper 5. more sustainable 6. fresher 7. safer 8. more concerned 9. more expensive 10. easier 11. more basic 12. thinner 13. closer 14. more harmful 15. flatter 16. farther/further

Exercise B.

- Have students work individually to complete the sentences with comparatives.
- Check answers as a class by writing the forms on the board and encouraging students to check their own answers. Have students correct their answers as necessary.

Answer Key

1. safer 2. healthier 3. more electricity 4. more nutrients 5. more variety 6. fewer chemicals

IDEAS FOR... Grammar Review

The Independent Student Handbook on pages 216 and 217 provides a summary of comparative forms.

Exercise C.

- Explain to students that they are to combine ideas from two sentences into a single comparison statement.
- Monitor students as they work, providing assistance as needed.
- Check answers as a class.

Answer Key

Possible answers:
1. Mega Corporate Farm is farther/further away than Johnson's Farm./Johnson's Farm is closer than Mega Corporate Farm. **2.** Local farms are more sustainable than corporate farms./Corporate farms are less sustainable than local farms. **3.** Food from local farms is more expensive than food from corporate farms./Food from corporate farms is less expensive/cheaper than food from local farms. **4.** Organic produce is more expensive than non-organic produce./Non-organic produce is less expensive/cheaper than organic produce. **5.** Large corporate farms use more fertilizer than small, local farms./Small, local farms use less fertilizer than large corporate farms.

Exercise D.

- Before students write their sentences, refer them back to page 95 and to the Independent Student Handbook on pages 216 and 217. Make sure they understand the difference between comparatives with adjectives and nouns.
- Have students write their sentences individually.
- Put students into pairs to review their sentences. Remind them of the steps they take when they do "peer evaluation" of one another's sentences before they write their final drafts at the end of the unit.

Answer Key

Answers will vary.

IDEAS FOR... Presenting Grammar

After exercise **D**, ask students to brainstorm about their favorite adjectives. Perhaps they are words like *awesome, brilliant,* or *cool.* What are the comparative forms?

Writing Skill: Using Synonyms to Avoid Repetition

Encourage students to use synonyms to avoid repetition in their writing. Although students are familiar with ordinary dictionaries, a *thesaurus* may be new to them. Present it as a special kind of dictionary that lists words by their relationship to other words such as *synonyms* (words that have a similar meaning) or *antonyms* (words that mean the opposite). Point out that synonyms often have slightly different shades of meaning, so one word can't always be used to replace another.

If using a thesaurus is new to your students, use exercise **E** as a homework assignment. Suggest that students explore both a print version such as Roget's Thesaurus and an online version such as http://thesaurus.com/

During the next class, check the synonyms for the underlined words. Is the meaning close to the original?

Answer Key

Possible answers:
1. put together/construct/assemble
2. learned/found out; parts/components
3. discovered; directions/guidelines; for creating/fabricating
4. traveled; to obtain; which he required

Exercise F. | Using Synonyms

- Have students work individually or in pairs to write their sentences. Suggest that students use a thesaurus.
- Walk around the room, providing assistance as necessary.
- Ask for volunteers to read out their sentences.

Writing Task: Drafting
(page 98)

Exercise A. | Brainstorming

- Remind students that brainstorming is a useful first step for gathering ideas before writing.
- Ask students to work in pairs to quickly write *pros* (advantages) and *cons* (disadvantages) of buying local and non-local food.
- Walk around the class as students work, and help them with ideas as needed.

Exercise B. | Planning

- Go over the steps in this exercise.
- Remind students that complete sentences are not necessary at this stage and that it is more important to focus on their ideas. Point out that students will have stronger arguments if all their advantages can be supported with examples.
- Allow time for students to work individually to write their lists.
- Walk around and monitor students' work. Provide assistance as needed.

Exercise C. | Draft 1

As students write their sentences, walk around and offer assistance as needed. Refrain from any type of error correction at this point.

Writing Task: Revising and Editing *(page 99)*

Exercise D. | Peer Evaluation

- Go over the steps in the evaluation process to make sure students know what to do.
- Remind students to read mostly for ideas and to be sure to give some positive feedback to their partner.
- Have students use the steps on page 99 to help them read their partner's work. Ensure that both members of the pair have equal time to give feedback.

Exercise E. | Draft 2

- Walk around and monitor students as they work. Provide assistance as needed.
- Remind students to use the feedback they got from their partner when writing their second draft.

Exercise F. | Editing Practice

- Go over the information in the box.
- Allow time for students to work individually to find and correct the errors in the sentences.
- Check the answers by asking students to read out the correct sentences and explain the errors.

Answer Key

1. Organic food is usually **more expensive** than non-organic food.
2. Fast food is **cheaper** than fresh fruits and vegetables.
3. Corporations use more fuel **than** local farms.
4. Fresh food is also **better** for you than fast food.
5. Corporate farms are usually **bigger** than local farms.
6. I feel **healthier** when I eat well.
7. Fresh food has more vitamins and minerals **than** fast food.
8. The supermarket is **farther/further** from my house than the neighborhood grocery store.

Writing Task: Editing
(page 100)

Exercise G. | Editing Checklist

- Go over the sentences in the editing checklist.
- Allow time for students to read and edit their work.

Exercise H. | Final Draft

Have students complete their final draft, and then collect their work.

TIP You can use students' sentences to collect (anonymous) examples of good sentences and common errors for the next class.

Unit Quiz

- Students can work in groups to answer the questions.
- Encourage students to refer back to the relevant pages of the unit to find the answers.
- To do the quiz as a competition, you can have students work in teams.

Answer Key

1. grains
2. century
3. iron, copper
4. Scanning
5. locavores
6. greenhouse gas emissions
7. comparative
8. Synonyms

IDEAS FOR... Further Research

People who care about the sources of the food they eat and about the environment prefer wild-caught to farm-raised fish. Students can explore the pros and cons of this topic by searching on the keyword *aquaculture*, meaning "fish farming."

Future Living

Academic Track: Science/Sociology

Academic Pathways   Lesson A: Understanding pronoun reference
                                    Evaluating a writer's attitude
                 Lesson B: Understanding a multimodal text
                 Lesson C: Using pronouns to avoid repetition
                                      Writing sentences about the future

Unit Theme

While it is difficult to make predictions about the future, several technologies under development now are likely to be important. Scientists are also investigating ways to move beyond Earth, perhaps by colonizing Mars.

Unit 6 explores the topic of the future as it relates to:

– predictions
– new technologies and daily life

– the challenges of colonizing Mars
– a typical day in 2050

Think and Discuss *(page 101)*

5 mins

- Ask students about some ways in which older people need help in their daily lives. For example, sometimes they need assistance in carrying things. How is the robot helping the woman in the photograph? (Possible answer: The robot has a shopping basket on its "arm" and can talk, so it can give advice. Perhaps the robot keeps track of what the woman buys and how much it costs.)

- Discuss question 1 as a class. Start by asking students to think back in time. When students' parents were their age, did they have cell phones and the Internet? Did their grandparents have television when they were young? When did airplanes become common? Then ask the class to move forward to guess what life will be like 50 or 100 years from now.

- Discuss question 2. Have volunteers share their opinions. Ask students to explain and justify their opinions. What has influenced their ideas? (Possible answer: Some students may be science fiction fans, while others might follow space exploration.)

Exploring the Theme

15 mins

(pages 102–103)

The opening spread features a photograph of a man talking with a robotic head.

- Before students answer the questions, ask them to quickly skim the titles of the texts on pages 102 and 103. How are they different? (Answer: The text on

102 has past predictions, and the text on 103 has present predictions about life in 2025.)

- Ask students to read the predictions on page 102. Which were correct and which were wrong?

- Have students discuss the predictions about 2025 in small groups. Which do they think are likely to happen and which seem unlikely? Students should provide reasons to support their opinions.

- Ask the class about the scene in the picture. What could the man and the robot be talking about? Do you think they could discuss any topic or only topics with predictable answers that have been programmed into the robot? (Possible answers: Maybe the man and the robot share an interest in a topic such as history or art.)

Answer Key

A1. The predictions about television, mobile phones, and digital photographs were correct.
A2. The predictions about telephones, flying machines (airplanes), and computers were incorrect.
B1. Electric cars, solar energy, and recording memories are all possible to some extent, as are robots with limited functions.
B2. Robots having rights seems unlikely.

> **TIP**   A time capsule is a container of objects that is meant to be stored and opened years in the future as a way of letting future historians and archaeologists understand what people valued at this time. If the class had to fill a time capsule with 10 things to be opened in 2050, what would those things be?

Preparing to Read *(page 104)*

30 mins

WARM-UP

The Lesson A target vocabulary is presented through two different tasks: a matching exercise and a sentence-completion activity. Students are asked to get meaning from context.

Exercise A. | Building Vocabulary

- Point out ways to use context to guess meaning:
  a) look at the meaning of any prefixes or suffixes;
  b) guess what part of speech the word is; and
  c) look at the key words in the sentence or previous sentence for clues to the definition.

- Have students find the blue words in the reading passage and then match the sentence parts to make definitions.

- Check the answers by asking volunteers to read out a sentence each.

- Point out the **Word Partners** box. Ask students to suggest sentences using each of these phrases. For example, *Robots are programmed with artificial intelligence so that they demonstrate some characteristics of the human mind.*

Vocabulary Notes

For instance and *for example* can be used interchangeably to introduce an example of the topic under discussion. Both phrases typically occur at the start of a sentence and are followed by a comma.

Answer Key

1. e 2. d 3. b 4. a 5. c

Exercise B. | Building Vocabulary

- Ask students to locate the words in the passage and guess their meaning from context. Allow time for students to work individually to complete the sentences and then compare answers in pairs.
- Check answers as a class.

Answer Key

1. temperature 2. network 3. keep track of 4. pattern
5. link

Exercise C. | Using Vocabulary

- Students apply the new vocabulary items by answering questions in which the new words are the key terms.

- After students complete the task individually, have them compare answers in pairs.

- Check answers by asking for volunteers to share their ideas with the class.

Answer Key

Possible answers:
1. Answers will vary.
2. I keep track of the news by going online/reading the newspaper/watching TV.
3. I see stripes/plaid/polka dots/checks/flowers/paisley.

TIP Ask students if they are familiar with the two main systems of measuring temperature. Most places in the world use the Celsius system, where 0° C is the freezing point and 100° the boiling point. However, the United States still uses the Fahrenheit system, where freezing happens at 32°F and water boils at 212°. Fortunately, there are many temperature converters online, so people don't have to remember the formula for doing it themselves!

Exercise D. | Brainstorming

Have students work in small groups and then share their ideas with the class.

Answer Key

Possible answers:
Technologies That Make Life Easier: cruise control on cars, smartphones, air conditioning
Technologies That Make Life More Fun: computer games, YouTube, e-cards, iPods

Exercise E. | Predicting

- Explain the exercise: Students scan the reading passage, looking for and underlining sentences with the auxiliary verb *will*. Explain or elicit that *will* signals the sentence is about the future. Point out that all the paragraphs except A have *will* sentences.

- Note: Students will check their predictions later, in exercise **A** on page 107.

track **2-01** Ask students to read the passage. Explain that the vocabulary definitions in the footnotes at the bottom of pages 105 and 106 will help them understand the reading.

Overview of the Reading

The passage describes technologies that are already in use to a limited extent but that could radically change homes in the future. People will have a more interactive role with their homes and appliances that use RFID chips and OLED digital screens. These "smart" appliances and equipment will inventory available food and keep track of human preferences for meals, temperature, amount of daylight, and décor. In addition, sociable robots will do housework, take care of dependent family members, and interact in human-like ways.

IDEAS FOR... Checking Visual Literacy

Have students look at the image of Dubai on page 105. Ask what they know about the city. Have any of them ever been there? Only a few decades ago, Dubai was a trading post on the eastern desert of the Arabian peninsula. Due to massive oil wealth and its favorable position for transportation on the crossroads of several continents, Dubai flourished and grew rapidly. Much of the building consists of climate-controlled skyscrapers, including the world's tallest building. Some people think this is the housing of the future. Ask the class if any of them would like to live in such a building and why.

For more information on Dubai, including pictures of its architecture and culture, visit http://travel.nationalgeographic.com/travel/city-guides/dubai-united-arab-emirates/

IDEAS FOR... Expansion

Four different kinds of robots are depicted on pages 101, 102, 106, and 108. If students would like to see more pictures of robots, suggest they go to the photo essay with the source article for these readings at http://ngm.nationalgeographic.com/2011/08/robots/robots-photography

---

Understanding the Reading *(page 107)*

45 mins

Exercise A. | Understanding the Gist

Check students' predictions in exercise **E** on page 104. Did they guess the general idea correctly?

Answer Key

The answer is c. The word *home* is not mentioned until paragraph B, but paragraph A clearly establisnes a setting that is neither a school nor an office.

Exercise B. | Identifying Main Ideas

- Although readers are looking for main ideas, an effective strategy is to scan for key words such as *ambient intelligence, RFID,* and *OLED.*

- Have students complete the task either individually or in pairs.

- Check the answers as a class.

Answer Key

1. E 2. C 3. D 4. H 5. G

Exercise C. | Identifying Key Details

- Students use information from the text to decide if the information is true (T) or false (F). You may want to ask students to correct the false statements.

- Allow time for students to complete the exercise individually before comparing answers in pairs.

- Check the answers as a class.

Answer Key

1. T
2. F (RFID chips are already used today for keeping track of pets and farm animals.)
3. F (People will change their wall patterns using OLED technology.)
4. T
5. T
6. F (Robots will soon be intelligent and sociable like humans.)

Exercise D. | Critical Thinking: Evaluating Attitude

- Have students read the **CT Focus** box carefully, pointing out clues about whether the author's attitude toward the subject is either positive or negative. In the opening paragraph, for example, the writer sets a pleasant tone and uses positive words such as *perfect* and *favorite*. Throughout the passage, the writer stresses the advantages of the new technology as though everyone would appreciate such practical features.

- Have students discuss their view of the author's attitude with a partner, indicating whether they agree with it or not.

- Discuss the issues as a class.

Answer Key

positive (optimistic)
The description makes life sound pleasant.
The writer makes these devices sound practical (useful).
Answers to the last questions will vary.

Exercise E. | Personalizing

- Allow time for students to discuss the questions in small groups.

- Discuss the answers as a class.

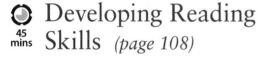

Developing Reading Skills *(page 108)*

45 mins

Reading Skill: Understanding Pronoun Reference

Go over the information in the box. If necessary, review the difference between subject and object pronouns.

Exercise A. | Matching

track 2-02

- Explain the task: Students practice identifying subject and object pronouns and drawing arrows to their antecedents.

- Have students complete the exercise individually and then compare answers in pairs.

- Check the answers as a class by asking volunteers to write the sentences on the board, adding the underlining and arrows.

Answer Key

They = Engineers	it = Wakamaru
It = Wakamaru	it = Wakamaru
them = words	them = family members

Exercise B. | Understanding Pronoun Reference

- Explain that the task is to go back to the reading passage and identify the antecedent of each of the underlined pronouns.

- Point out that reading comprehension tasks on standardized tests often have at least one pronoun reference question.

- After students complete the task, check the answers as a class.

Answer Key

1. them = RFID chips
2. they = RFID chips
3. it = the OLED technology
4. They = sociable robots

Viewing: Colonizing Mars
(page 109)

30 mins

Overview of the Video

Although there have been several unmanned missions to Mars, to date there have been no attempts to send people there. It has been considered too risky and too expensive.

Dr. Bob Zubrin disagrees. Zubrin is an aerospace engineer and author of many books advocating manned missions to Mars. He is also head of the Mars Society and a non-governmental group (NGO) called Mars Direct. This NGO believes there are ways to put people on Mars in an affordable way.

Having humans on Mars poses many problems because of the cold temperature of the planet and the lack of oxygen and liquid water. Zubrin and his colleague Dr. Chris McKay believe they can solve these problems by warming up Mars's atmosphere with greenhouse gases and by using cyano bacteria, the same organism that once created oxygen on Earth.

Meanwhile, other scientists continue to study Mars and learn more about its resources.

To learn more about the views and activities of the Mars Society, visit **http://en.wikipedia.org/wiki/Mars_Society**

Before Viewing

Exercise A. | Using a Dictionary

- Students become familiar with some of the key vocabulary in the video by looking up the words in the box and then completing the definitions.

- Discuss the answers as a class.

Answer Key

1. mission
2. colonize
3. ambitious
4. credible
5. frontier
6. restore

Exercise B. | Predicting

- Students work in pairs to answer the questions.

- Open the discussion up to the whole class, and have volunteers share their ideas and opinions.

While Viewing

Exercise A.

- Ask students to read the statements silently.

- Play the video. Ask students to think about their answers to the questions in the Predicting exercise in Before Viewing and to circle **T** or **F** for each of the statements.

After Viewing

Exercise A.

- Have students work in pairs to discuss and compare their answers. Ask volunteers to correct the false statement.

- Play the video again. If necessary, refer students to the video script on page 206.

- Point out that statement 4 is understood to mean that some scientists—such as the ones featured in the video—believe humans could live on Mars in the future. Not all scientists agree on this point.

Answer Key

1. T
2. T
3. F (We are not certain that there was never any life on Mars.)
4. T

Exercise B. | Synthesizing

- Explain that students are to consider how the technologies from the reading might be useful for living on Mars.

- Have students discuss the issue in pairs or small groups.

- Monitor students while they are working, and identify the types of errors they are making. When students finish their discussions, go over some of the things that caused them difficulties.

Answer Key

Possible answers:
Robots could perform many tasks in that cold, inhospitable environment.
Computer networks would be necessary to control temperature, oxygen, and atmospheric pressure in the domes where people would live.

Preparing to Read

(pages 110–111)

30 mins

WARM-UP

The Lesson B target vocabulary is presented in two matching exercises, one of which includes an original paragraph with more information about Mars and the other based on the reading passage on pages 112–113.

Exercise A. | Building Vocabulary

- Have students read the paragraph, find the words in blue, and circle the words they're not sure about.
- Have students try to guess the meanings of the words from context and then do the matching exercise.
- Check answers as a class.

Answer Key

1. c 2. e 3. a 4. b 5. d

Exercise B. | Building Vocabulary

- Have students work individually to match the sentence parts to create definitions.
- Before checking answers as a class, ask students to compare their answers with a partner.
- Draw students' attention to the **Word Partners** box.
- Remind students to list the word partners in their vocabulary notebooks.

Answer Key

1. d 2. c 3. e 4. a 5. b

IDEAS FOR... **Expansion**

As a follow-up to exercise **B** and preparation for the reading, have students draw simple diagrams of the oxygen cycle. Plants produce oxygen through photosynthesis in sunlight. At the same time, plants take in carbon dioxide. Humans and other animals breathe in oxygen and give off carbon dioxide, so there is an endless cycle. This explains why it would be so important to have plants on Mars, which has mostly carbon dioxide in its thin atmosphere. Many good diagrams of the process are available online under *diagram oxygen cycle*.

Exercise C. | Using Vocabulary

- Draw students' attention to the **Word Usage** box, which provides examples of the noun and adjective forms of *average*.
- Give an example of your own for the first item if necessary.
- While students share their sentences with a partner, circulate through the classroom listening unobtrusively to students' interactions. Make sure that both partners are participating equally.

Exercise D. | Predicting

- Have students use the title, pictures, and numbered captions to predict the reading topic.
- Note: Students will check their predictions later, in exercise A on page 114.

track **2-03** Ask students to read the article. Explain that the vocabulary definitions in the footnotes at the bottom of pages 112 and 113 will help them understand the reading.

Overview of the Reading

The reading passage is considered multimodal because it contains text and an illustration numbered with corresponding captions describing a sequence of steps in colonizing Mars. In a way, the illustration is also a visual timeline because on the left, an astronaut is shown landing on an unmodified, barren planet. On the far right—1,000 years later—a person looks at a landscape that has been transformed or *terraformed* to look more like Earth.

The source for the reading and graphics is an article by Robert Kunzig, the senior environmental editor for National Geographic, in the February 2010 issue, available online at **http://ngm.nationalgeographic. com/big-idea/07/mars**. The article describes a long, gradual process of using greenhouse gases—a problem associated with global warming on Earth—to raise the temperature on Mars so that the atmosphere changes. This would also change ice to liquid water and eventually permit plants to grow and produce oxygen.

Understanding the Reading *(page 114)*

Exercise A. | Understanding the Gist

Check students' predictions in exercise **D** on page 111.

Answer Key

The correct answer is c. Item b is incorrect because travel to Mars is only mentioned as a supporting detail. Item b isn't correct because there is no mention of an average day on Mars.

Exercise B. | Identifying Key Details

- Have students complete the task individually and then compare answers in pairs.

- Check answers as a class by asking volunteers to write the missing words and paragraph letters on the board.

Answer Key

1. B, liquid water
2. C, Earth's environment
3. J, breathe
4. E, six
5. C, factories, greenhouse
6. I, nuclear power, wind turbines

Exercise C. | Sequencing

- Ask students to work individually to use dates and numbers from the drawing and text to put the events in order. Point out that on this time line, the present appears on the far left and projections into the future stretch to 1,000 years from now on the right side of the time line.

- Compare answers as a class.

Answer Key

d, a, c, b

Exercise D. | Understanding Pronoun Reference

- Draw students' attention to the **Strategy** box, which provides clues for finding the nouns that pronouns refer to.

- Ask students to work individually to scan to find the sentences in the passage and then identify the antecedent. Point out that there are two extra nouns in the right-hand column

- Check answers as a class.

Answer Key

1. b 2. d 3. e

Exercise E. | Critical Thinking: Synthesizing/Evaluating

- Put students into small groups to discuss the questions.

- Discuss the answers as a class.

Answer Key

Possible answers:
1. Generally, the video and reading are in close agreement. The reading passage gives a time frame and much more detail on the steps involved in the process. It also introduces the idea of *terraforming*.
2. Individual answers will vary, but interested students can research a Dutch plan, Mars One, to have human settlements on Mars by 2023 at http://mars-one. com/en/

> **TIP** Welcome diverse responses to the Synthesizing/Evaluating questions. For questions that include "Why?", encourage students to support their opinions with reasons or examples.

IDEAS FOR... Expansion

The term *terraforming* first occurred in science fiction literature as did many other ideas about colonizing space. Ask if any students are science fiction fans. Perhaps they know the works of Isaac Asimov, who wrote of encasing cities in *Caves of Steel* and colonizing other planets in the Foundation series.

---

45 mins

Exploring Written English *(pages 115–117)*

In this lesson, students go through the process of writing sentences about a typical day in the year 2050. The lesson starts with a review of conjunctions that connect information in sentences and then follows the steps in the writing process. In the final sentences, students write about their home, work, family, travel or entertainment in 2050.

Exercise A. | Language for Writing

- Go over the information in the box.

- Take this opportunity to review the difference between *clauses,* which have their own subject and verb, and *phrases,* which lack one of these.

- Have students complete the task individually and then compare answers in pairs.

- Check the answers as a class.

Answer Key

1. so 2. and 3. and 4. so 5. so 6. but 7. but 8. so

Exercise B.

- Make sure students understand the task: They are to rewrite each pair of sentences as one, using appropriate conjunctions. Put the example on the board and show how the pronoun (*They*) and the auxiliary verb (*can*) have been omitted.

- Check the answers by asking volunteers to write the sentences on the board.

Answer Key

1. PR2 can take care of elderly people **and** deliver mail.
2. PR2 cooks, **but** it doesn't communicate./PR2 cooks **but** doesn't communicate.
3. Wakamaru knows 10,000 Japanese words, **so** it is able to communicate with people.
4. There is not enough oxygen on Mars, **so** humans cannot breathe there.

IDEAS FOR...   Grammar Review

The Independent Student Handbook on page 213 provides a brief overview of coordinating conjunctions.

Exercise C.

- Students work in pairs to think of future objects. They describe how the items will look and work, using conjunctions.

- Bring the class together and have each pair talk about one of their "inventions."

Answer Key

Answers will vary.

Writing Skill: Using Pronouns to Avoid Repetition

Point out that repeating the same word over and over in writing is boring for the reader and can be avoided using synonyms—as in Unit 5—or pronouns. Remind students that pronouns need to agree with the noun in number and gender.

Exercise D.

- Allow time for students to work individually. Walk around the class and offer help as needed.

- Students who finish early can compare answers in pairs.

- Check the answers as a class.

Answer Key

1. RFID chips will keep track of the food in your cabinets, and **they** will tell you when it's time to go to the store.
2. People on survey missions to Mars will build domes and live in **them**.
3. People will terraform Mars and make **it** more like Earth.
4. Even after a thousand years, people won't be able to breathe on Mars, so **they** will have to use breathing equipment.
5. Mars doesn't have any oxygen, but plants will slowly add **it** to the atmosphere over many years.

Exercise E.

- Ask students to work individually to identify the nouns that correspond to the underlined pronouns.

- Check the answers as a class.

Answer Key

1. the robots, people 2. the domes 3. the colors

Writing Task: Drafting

(page 118)

Exercise A. | Brainstorming

- Have students work in pairs to quickly write down some ideas about a typical day in 2050.
- Walk around the class as students write their ideas. Monitor their work and provide assistance as needed.

Exercise B. | Planning

- Go over the steps in the exercise.
- Remind students that complete sentences are not necessary at this stage and that it is more important to focus on their ideas than on grammar or spelling.
- Point out that the details need to relate to and support the main idea.
- Walk around and monitor students as they work. Provide assistance as needed.
- Select some good ideas and read them aloud without mentioning whose they are. Discuss them with the class.

Exercise C. | Draft 1

As students write their sentences, walk around and offer help if asked. Refrain from any type of error correction at this point.

Writing Task: Revising and Editing *(page 119)*

Exercise D. | Peer Evaluation

- Remind students that peer evaluation will help make them better writers.
- Go over the three steps in the exercise and make sure students know what to do.

Exercise E. | Draft 2

- Walk around and monitor students as they work. Provide assistance as needed.
- Remind students to use the feedback they got from their partner.

Exercise F. | Editing Practice

- The purpose of this exercise is to give students additional practice in editing for grammar in preparation for using the **Editing Checklist** for their second draft. Focusing on grammar and punctuation at this stage prepares students to write their final draft.
- Go over the information in the box.
- Allow time for students to work individually to find and correct the problems.
- Check the answers by asking students to read out the correct sentences and explain the errors.

Answer Key

1. People will live on Mars someday, **but** it is too expensive to travel there now.
2. Mars is too cold for human visitors, **so** they will need to warm it up.
3. Robots will take care of children, **and** they will do housework/Robots will take care of children **and** do homework.
4. A trip to Mars sounds amazing, **but** I would not like to live there!
5. Smart appliances will buy food **and** cook dinner.
6. We might have flying cars in 2050, **so** there will probably be fewer cars on our roads.
7. In the future, you will put a language chip in your brain, **so** you won't have to study foreign languages.

Writing Task: Editing

(page 120)

> **TIP** Final drafts usually focus on details such as spelling and punctuation. If students are working on a computer, ask them to set the spelling and grammar tools.

Exercise G. | Editing Checklist

- Go over the sentences in the editing checklist.
- Allow time for students to read and edit their work.
- Ask for some examples of each type of error.

Exercise H. | Final Draft

Have students complete their final draft, and then collect their work.

> **TIP** You can use students' sentences to collect (anonymous) examples of good sentences and common errors for the next class.

Unit Quiz

- Students can work in groups to answer the questions.
- Encourage students to refer back of the relevant pages of the unit to find the answers.
- To do the quiz as a competition, you can have students work in teams.

Answer Key

1. prediction, sun
2. example
3. robots
4. earlier
5. mission
6. plant
7. Earth
8. contrast/contrasting idea

IDEAS FOR...   **Further Discussion**

When people volunteer for the Mars One mission, they will leave for Mars and never come back to Earth. Have students talk about this idea in small groups. How would they feel about going to another world? What or who would they want to take with them? What kinds of adjustments would they have to make?

Exploration and Discovery

Academic Track: Interdisciplinary

Academic Pathways: Lesson A: Understanding prefixes
Evaluating reasons
Lesson B: Understanding an explanatory text and infographic
Lesson C: Linking examples and reasons
Writing sentences to give reasons

Unit Theme

Although most of Earth has been explored, there are still areas with things to discover and learn about. Explorers can learn about past expeditions, discover new animals and plants, and dive into underwater caves to investigate an extreme environment with clues to the past.

Unit 7 explores the topic of exploration as it relates to:

– some important events in exploration
– a recreation of Stanley's famous expedition
– discovering the world's smallest primate
– diving into blue holes in the Bahamas

Think and Discuss *(page 121)*

5 mins

- Ask students to describe the picture. What is the setting for this photo? Refer them to the caption. (Answer: A diver explores an underwater cave in the Yucatán peninsula of Mexico. This type of cave is called a blue hole, something rare that occurs in places such as the Bahamas, the Red Sea, off the Great Barrier Reef in Australia, and in the Yucatán.) Why is the presence of a cow skull unusual? (Answer: Normally, bone would decay over time, but blue holes have no oxygen, so things are preserved.) Ask: *What is the diver doing?* (Answer: The diver is writing on a clipboard, so he is probably a researcher.)

- Discuss question 1 as a class. Start by brainstorming as many names as students can think of and writing them on the board. (Possible answers: Ibn Battuta, Zheng He, Francis Drake, James Cook, Roald Amundsen, Vasco da Gama, David Livingstone, Ferdinand Magellan)

- Discuss question 2. (Possible answers: Some people are exploring extreme environments on Earth such as the deep Mariana Trench in the Pacific Ocean or remote parts of the Amazon Basin. Astronauts are exploring life in space, and astrophysicists are exploring outer space with space probes.)

Exploring the Theme *(pages 122–123)*

15 mins

- Ask students to look at the pictures and the time line and read about each historic moment.

- For question 1, ask who Livingstone was and what he was famous for. (Answer: He was a British explorer who was looking for—but didn't find—the source of the Nile River.) Why was Stanley searching for him? (Answer: Livingstone had been missing for six years.) Where did he find him? (Answer: He found him in a village called Ujiji in what is now Tanzania.)

Answer Key

1. Stanley found Livingstone. **2.** They were each solo "firsts"—Tereshkova the first woman in space and Cameron the first person to go alone to Earth's deepest spot. **3.** (Possible answers: the moon landing, the discovery of America, finding Machu Picchu)

IDEAS FOR... Expansion

Have students research famous explorers in their part of the world. Who were these people? When did they live? What did they find? Suggest that students search on keywords *famous explorers* and refine the search by adding a place name, e.g., Australia.

Preparing to Read *(page 124)*

30 mins

WARM-UP

The Lesson A target vocabulary is presented through an exercise in which students see the words in context. They complete sentences by choosing the correct option.

Exercise A. | Building Vocabulary

- Have students find the words in the reading and use the other words around them to guess their meanings. Then have them complete the sentences using one of the two given words or phrases.

- Allow time for students to work individually or in pairs.

- Check the answers by asking volunteers to read out a sentence each.

- Point out the **Word Link** box. If students have their dictionaries, ask them to work in small groups and look at words starting with *re-*. Can they decide between words where *re-* means "again" and where it is just part of the spelling? Time permitting, this could be a competitive game. Note that the verb *recreate* (to make or do something again) is sometimes spelled with a hyphen: *re-create*.

Vocabulary Notes

Traditionally, *journalists* such as Henry Stanley were people whose job was to gather and report the news. *Print journalists* now work for newspapers or magazines, while *broadcast journalists* work in radio or television. The Internet has expanded the role of journalists to include people who publish or blog online or are involved in editing or photographing the news. Increasingly, news stories are reported from the scene by witnesses who use cell phones to photograph and communicate what is actually happening in real time.

TIP A *series* is a set of TV programs that are connected from one episode to the next. Typically, an episode has an unresolved issue toward the end so that viewers are eager to find out what happens in the next episode. The reading passage is based on an eight-part reality series called *Expedition Africa: Stanley & Livingstone* that was shown on the History Channel.

Answer Key

1. occupation
2. journalist
3. especially
4. finally
5. search
6. source
7. series
8. moment
9. recreate
10. camp

Exercise B. | Using Vocabulary

After students discuss the questions in pairs, ask for volunteers to share their answers with the entire class.

Answer Key

Possible answers:
1. Police officers, firefighters, soldiers
2. Answers will vary.
3. Newspapers, TV news programs, the Web. Some sources are more factual or less biased than others.

IDEAS FOR... Expansion

Many English-language newspapers throughout the world are available online. For homework, have students explore the news on one day in five different newspapers and report on the differences and similarities in the sources. For links, see: http://www.inkdrop.net/dave/news.html

---

Exercise C. | Brainstorming

- Give students a minute or two to think of ideas in pairs.

- Lead a class discussion about the difficulties faced by explorers during Stanley's time.

Answer Key

Possible answers:
no roads, lack of communication (without telephones, postal service, etc.), dangerous animals and plants, difficulty finding food and clean water

Exercise D. | Predicting

- Students are usually asked to predict the main topic of the passage. However, this time the focus is on the author.

- Several clues help establish who the writer is. First, the name of the author is given in the picture. Second, the reading on page 126 consists of journal entries organized according to days of the expedition. The expression "in (someone's) footsteps" means that you are doing something that another person did before you—in this case, making a journey.

- Refer students back to the drawing and text on page 122, which will help them understand the sentences on the photo on page 125.

- Note: Students will check their predictions later, in exercise **A** on page 127.

Ask students to read the passage. Explain that the vocabulary definitions in the footnotes at the bottom of pages 125 and 126 will help them understand the reading.

 track 2-04

Overview of the Reading

Mireya Mayor was part of a four-person team that retraced Stanley's 1871 expedition as part of a TV series. The team started in Zanzibar in East Africa and crossed mountains and plains in Tanzania to reach Lake Tanganyika. The expedition accepted the challenge to make the journey under the original conditions, but they took a route somewhat different from Stanley's—going over the Uluguru Mountains instead of around them. The team completed the journey in a month instead of the nine months it took Stanley.

Henry Morton Stanley was born in Wales, but traveled to the U.S. as a young man. Always adventuresome, he served in the Civil War and later went on an expedition to the Ottoman Empire. He got funded to search for Livingston and started with 200 porters to carry equipment and supplies. Soon, disease and rough tropical conditions reduced the size of the group. Despite these problems, Stanley carried on and finally found Livingstone. Together, they established that there was no connection between Lake Tanganyika and the Nile. In later years, Stanley wrote about his exploration of the Congo River.

Understanding the Reading *(page 127)*

45 mins

 Exercise A. | Understanding the Gist

Check students' predictions in exercise **D** on page 124. Did they guess the writer of the passage?

Answer Key

The correct answer is item c. The writer is Mireya Mayor, who recreated Henry Stanley's journey. Option b refers to Livingstone, who searched for the source of the Nile. Option a is about Stanley, who searched for Livingstone in 1871.

Exercise B. | Identifying Main Ideas

- Have students work individually or in pairs to scan the passage for the main ideas and to identify the paragraph in which they are found.
- Check the answers as a class.

Answer Key

1. H 2. C 3. F 4. J 5. A

Exercise C. | Identifying Key Details

- Tell students to scan the passage again, this time to find details to complete the sentences. Suggest that they note the paragraph in which they find information as this will help them in the next exercise.
- After students complete the task individually, ask them to compare answers in pairs.
- Check answers as a class.

Answer Key

a. million years old (paragraph F) **b.** bones of dead animals (paragraph G) **c.** 4,200 (paragraph E) **d.** phones (paragraph C) **e.** grass (paragraph G) **f.** snakes (paragraph I) **g.** toenail (paragraph I) **h.** nine, 900 (paragraph D)

Exercise D. | Sequencing

- Students put the sentences in the previous exercise in the correct order.
- Note that sentence d is identified as the first event and that it occurs in paragraph C.
- Check the answers as a class.

Answer Key

Order from top to bottom: 4, 5, 3, 1, 6, 7, 8, 2

Exercise E. | Critical Thinking: Evaluating Reasons

- Draw students' attention to the **CT Focus** box, which suggests that sometimes a writer explicitly gives reasons, but at other times it is up to the reader to infer the author's reasons.
- Students work in pairs to answer the questions.
- Check the answers as a class by asking volunteers to share their ideas.

Answer Key

1. The goal was to survive Stanley's journey, under the same conditions.
2. Other reasons included facing a difficult challenge and creating a TV series.
3. The sponsors probably limited the risks.
4. Mayor and her team knew the route and the pitfalls.
5. Answers will vary.

Developing Reading Skills *(page 128)*

45 mins

Reading Skill: Understanding Prefixes

- Go over the information in the box.
- Remind students that recognizing common prefixes is a very important tool for decoding the meaning of unfamiliar words. The prefixes in this lesson are among the most frequently used, so learning them provides important clues to understanding new vocabulary.

track 2-05

Exercise A. | Understanding Prefixes

- Have students work individually to identify and underline words starting with prefixes.
- Put students into pairs to discuss the meanings of the underlined words.
- Check answers as a class.

Answer Key

1. unexplored (not explored) 2. misfortunes (bad luck)
3. returned (went back) 4. disappeared (went away/wasn't seen again) 5. unknown (not known) 6. retrace (go back over/do again)

Exercise B. | Identifying Prefixes

- Ask students to look in the reading passage for an example of each prefix. Then tell them to use their dictionaries to find two more examples for each.
- Check answers as a class. Ask for volunteers to write their dictionary words on the board.

Answer Key

1. *dis-*: *disappearance* (paragraph B)
2. *ex-*: *expeditions* (paragraph C) and *explains* (paragraph H)
3. *re-*: *recreate* (paragraph C)
4. *im-*: *impossible* (paragraphs D and F)
   Dictionary words will vary.

30 mins

Viewing: Madagascar Discovery *(page 129)*

Overview of the Video

Mireya Mayor went on an expedition to Madagascar—a large island off the coast of East Africa—to learn about lemurs, small members of the primate order. While there, the exploration team found a previously unknown lemur called a mouse lemur. The video notes some of the primate characteristics shared by this tiny lemur and humans: large brains, 10 fingers and toes with nails instead of claws, opposable thumbs, and forward-facing eyes with stereoscopic vision.

Mayor, an anthropologist with a Ph.D. in primatology, has had an interesting career track starting as a cheerleader and later serving as a National Geographic Emerging Explorer. For a video about her career and book, *Pink Boots and a Machete*, see http://events. nationalgeographic.com/events/video-gallery/115/

Before Viewing

Exercise A. | Using a Dictionary

- Students become familiar with some of the key vocabulary in the video by looking up the words in the box using them to complete the sentences.
- Check the answers as a class.

Vocabulary Notes

Biologists classify plants and animals by using *taxonomy*, a hierarchical set of categories that move from the most inclusive—the animal *kingdom*—down to the *species*, a category of similar animals that interbreed and produce viable offspring. Midway in the taxonomic system is the category called *order*. The *order* of primates includes humans, monkeys, apes, and lemurs.

Genus is a level higher than species that includes a variety of lemurs, but the mouse lemur in the video is a previously unknown *species*.

Answer Key

1. species **2.** identified **3.** primate **4.** surroundings

Exercise B. | Predicting

- Tell students to look at the photo, video title, and the vocabulary in exercise **A**. Ask: *What is the video about? Can you guess?*
- Come back to this once students have seen the video. How many students guessed correctly?

Answer Key

The correct answer is c. There is no mention of danger, so a is incorrect. Item b isn't correct because the team is there to find an unfamiliar animal—not to save endangered animals.

While Viewing

Exercise A.

- Ask students to read the questions in exercise **A** and to keep the questions in mind while watching the video.
- Play the video. Ask students to circle their answers as they watch.

Answer Key

1. T **2.** T **3.** F (Mouse lemurs drink water on leaves and branches.) **4.** T **5.** F (Another primate characteristic is eyes that face forward, not sideways.)

After Viewing

Exercise A.

After students compare and discuss their answers in While Viewing, check answers as a class. Ask volunteers to give the correct information for the false statements. If necessary, play the video again.

Exercise B. | Synthesizing

- By now, students are aware that Mireya Mayor is the writer of the first reading as well as the discoverer of the mouse lemur in the video. Based on her work as an explorer, have students think of adjectives to describe her personality.
- Students work in pairs to compare the two activities Mayor was involved in, giving reasons why they think one was more important than the other.
- Lead a class discussion about the issues raised in the activity.

Answer Key

Possible answers:
1. adventurous, brave, curious, capable, enthusiastic
2. Most people will probably think adding to scientific knowledge by discovering a new species is more important than recreating an expedition for a reality TV series.

Preparing to Read

(pages 130–131)

30 mins

WARM-UP

The Lesson B target vocabulary is presented in an activity that asks students to use context to guess the meanings of new words.

Exercise A. | Building Vocabulary

- Ask students to choose if they want to work individually or in pairs.

- Have students complete the task individually and then compare answers in pairs.

- Draw students' attention to the first **Word Partners** box, which focuses on *follow*. Ask for volunteers to choose one of the phrases and make up a sentence with the word partner.

- Ask students to read the second **Word Partners** box, which discusses some of the phrasal verbs associated with *run*. Ask students to look in their dictionaries and find the entries for *run across, run into*, and *run up against*. Can they think of their own sentence for each of the phrasals? Can they find other phrasal verbs with *run*? (Possible answers: run away, run through)

Answer Key

1. a 2. a 3. b 4. a 5. b 6. a 7. b 8. a 9. b 10. a

Exercise B. | Using Vocabulary

- Remind students to respond to the questions with complete sentences.

- While students share their sentences with a partner, circulate through the classroom listening unobtrusively to students' interactions.

Answer Key

Possible answers:
1. Scientists are searching for exoplanets that might support simple forms of life such as cyanobacteria.
2. It is extremely difficult to live in the desert, in places with extreme temperatures, and in isolated areas.
3. Answers will vary.
4. Rain forests are important because they support many kinds of plants, birds, and animals.

Exercise C. | Brainstorming

- The aim of this exercise is to activate students' background knowledge about relatively unexplored areas.

- Have students discuss the questions in pairs. Then ask volunteers to share their ideas with the class.

Answer Key

Possible answers:
Some places on Earth that are still mostly unexplored are caves and deserts, the Amazon rain forest, Antarctica, Greenland, and the Mariana Trench.

TIP To make the activity competitive, divide the class into two teams. Have each team write as many different ideas as they can think of in three minutes. Then compare lists, and the team with more ideas wins.

Exercise D. | Predicting

- Explain that students are going to use several sources to predict the content of the reading passage.

- Ask students to look at the pictures, captions, and first paragraph. Have them work individually to check their predictions.

- Students will check their predictions later, in exercise **A** on page 134.

 track 2-06 Ask students to read the article. Remind them that the vocabulary definitions in the footnotes at the bottom of page 133 are there to help them understand the reading.

Overview of the Reading

The passage describes the exploration of blue holes, inland underwater caves in the Bahamas. These deep caves are among the least explored places on Earth because diving in them is extremely dangerous. The passage describes some of the dangers in detail, as well as the scientific reasons divers risk their lives in this type of exploration. The oxygen-free environment at the bottom of blue holes preserves the skeletons of people and animals that fell into them long ago. Thus, scientists from many disciplines collect data unavailable elsewhere. In addition, bacteria that exist without oxygen are found in the caves, something that may have parallels in space environments.

The passage features an infographic, a visual representation of the context and layers of a blue hole. Blue holes are found inland, away from the sea as shown in the graphic. Encourage students to find the layers mentioned in the text to the left of the graphic. (Students will label the graphic in exercise C on page 134.)

National Geographic and Public Television's NOVA programming conducted a joint expedition to the Bahamas' blue holes. An hour-long film describing the scope of the exploration is at http://www.pbs.org/wgbh/nova/earth/extreme-cave-diving.html The film shows the guideline and discusses additional reasons why the diving risk is so great. These include several kinds of nitrogen narcosis, the danger of getting lost in side passages, debris falling on divers, and the need for rebreathing equipment to explore the depths.

IDEAS FOR... Expansion

The risks in exploring blue holes are real. Point out the caption on the main photograph about the death of the team's photographer. His photo gallery taken during the expedition illustrates many of the main points of the reading passage. Visit it at http://ngm.nationalgeographic.com/2010/08/bahamas-caves/skiles-photography

---

Understanding the Reading
(page 134)

Exercise A. | Understanding the Gist

Check students' predictions in exercise **D** on page 131.

Answer Key

1. All the topics should be checked except "how to preserve blue holes."
2. Paragraph C covers these topics: It is easy to get lost; they contain poisonous gas and bacteria; and they are very dark inside. The depth is mentioned in paragraph B.

Exercise B. | Identifying Key Ideas

- Students work individually to use words and phrases from the text to complete information. When they finish writing, ask them to compare answers with a partner and to correct them as necessary.
- Check the answers as a class.

Answer Key

1. A blue hole forms when the earth above it falls in.
2. The deepest hole is Dean's Blue Hole. It is 660 feet/200 meters deep.
3. The gas near the top of the blue hole can cause itching, dizziness, and death.
4. Divers follow a guideline in order not to get lost.

Exercise C. | Labeling a Diagram

- Ask students to use information from the reading passage to label the diagram of a blue hole. You might want to direct students to paragraph F, where most of the information can be found.
- A labeled version of the infographic is available at http://ngm.nationalgeographic.com/2010/08/bahamas-caves/caves-graphic

Answer Key

From top to bottom in order: rainwater; bacteria, Jupiter; salt water; Oxygen

Exercise D. | Critical Thinking: Evaluating Reasons

In pairs, students revisit the reading passage to find reasons to use in answering the questions.

Answer Key

Possible answers:
1. The layers of poisonous gases, the darkness which can cause divers to get lost, the amount of time it takes to dive deep, and the limited supply of oxygen divers have.
2. To learn about bacteria that may have existed long ago on Earth and other places in space and to get information about ancient life forms such as the remipede.

IDEAS FOR... Checking Comprehension

Ask more about Paragraph E. What kinds of bones and skeletons might scientists find? What would that tell them about life in prehistoric times? For example, today there are no crocodiles in the Bahamas, yet divers found crocodile skeletons in the blue holes.

Exercise E. | Synthesizing

- Have students discuss the questions in small groups. Expect individual opinions about the second question since it involves value judgments.
- Allow some time for a class discussion.

Answer Key

Possible answers:
1. Mayor and the divers are all willing to take risks to learn more about the environment. However, Mayor is sheltered from some risks because she travels with a film crew. The divers are each on their own in very risky circumstances.
2. Answers will vary.

Exploring Written English *(pages 135–137)*

45 mins

In this lesson, students go through the process of writing sentences about places they would like to explore. The lesson starts with a presentation of language for giving reasons for things you want to do and then follows the steps in the writing process. In the final sentences, the students write about a special place and why they want to go there.

Exercise A. | Language for Writing

• Go over the information in the box.

• Remind students that a clause has both a subject and a verb. Also point out that there is usually no comma before *because* in the middle of the sentence.

• Encourage students not to write complete sentences in the chart. The focus should be on ideas and not on grammar or spelling.

 TIP Write the chart on the board and use the last two example sentences from the Language for Writing box to illustrate the task. The left column should contain *explore Central America,* and the right column should have 1. *interested in Mayan history* and 2. *improve my Spanish language skills.*

Exercise B.

• Allow time for students to write their four sentences individually.

• Walk around as students write, and offer help or suggestions as needed. If necessary, ask questions to help students expand their ideas.

Writing Skill: Linking Examples and Reasons

A common theme in the writing lessons is avoiding redundancy and using a variety of phrases to make writing more interesting. Ways to link examples and reasons are modeled in a series of related sentences.

Exercise C. | Linking Ideas

• Make sure that everyone knows what to do. Students are to add words and phrases to five sentences to link them in a cohesive way.

• After students finish, check answers as a class.

Possible answers:
I would love to explore Australia because the national parks have so many interesting animals. In addition, I would like to see the Great Barrier Reef because I enjoy scuba diving. Another reason is because I want to visit the famous Sydney Opera House. Finally, I would love to travel around Australia because I really like hot weather!

Exercise D. | Linking Ideas

• Allow time for students to apply the technique from exercise **C** to the sentence pairs they wrote on page 136.

• Walk around and monitor students' work. Provide assistance as needed.

Writing Task: Drafting *(page 138)*

Exercise A. | Brainstorming

• Ask students to quickly write down all the places they would like to explore.

• Put students into pairs to discuss their ideas.

• When pairs finish their discussions, ask volunteers to tell the class where their partner would like to explore or learn more about.

Exercise B. | Planning

• Tell students to choose the place they want to write about and to include the four reasons that they want to explore this place.

• Allow time for students to work individually to follow the steps.

• Walk around the room, providing assistance as needed.

Exercise C. | Draft 1

• Ask volunteers to suggest other introductory sentences.

• As students write their sentences, walk around and offer help if asked. Refrain from any type of error correction at this point.

Writing Task: Revising and Editing *(page 139)*

Exercise D. | Peer Evaluation

- Have students use the three steps to help them read their partner's work. Note the emphasis on giving reasons for choosing the place and on linking ideas to avoid repetition. Explain that each sentence should include new information.
- Make sure that both members of the pair have equal time to give feedback.

Exercise E. | Draft 2

- Walk around and monitor students as they work. Provide assistance as needed.
- Remind students to use the feedback they got from their partner.

Exercise F. | Editing Practice

- Go over the information in the box.
- Allow time for students to work individually to find and correct the errors.
- Check the answers by asking students to read out the correct sentences and explain the errors.

Answer Key

1. I would like **to** visit the rain forests of the Amazon because they are full of different species.
2. I would love to explore New York City because **it** is full of interesting art and culture.
3. My brother and I would like to explore Russia **because** we are interested in Russian history.
4. My sister would like **to travel** to every continent because she loves to learn about different cultures.
5. My parents **would** like to go to Easter Island one day because they want to see the statues there.

Writing Task: Editing

(page 140)

> **TIP** Remind students that the first and second drafts usually focus on getting the ideas well organized and clearly presented. The final draft should focus on details such as grammar, spelling, and punctuation.

Exercise G. | Editing Checklist

- Go over the sentences in the editing checklist.
- Allow time for students to read and edit their work.

Exercise H. | Final Draft

Have students complete their final draft, and then collect their work.

Unit Quiz

- Students can work in groups to answer the questions.
- Encourage students to refer back to the relevant pages of the unit to find the answers.
- To do the quiz as a competition, you can have students work in teams.

Answer Key

1. deepest
2. Henry Stanley
3. prefix
4. primate
5. underwater cave
6. moon
7. because
8. addition

> **IDEAS FOR... Further Research**
>
> Suggest that students visit National Geographic's Explorers homepage at http://www.nationalgeographic.com/explorers/ to learn about young explorers and the places they are investigating. It may give the class ideas for projects that tie in with their own interests and studies. Time permitting, perhaps each student could do a brief presentation about a current expedition. Many of these places are not well known, so encourage them to show the locations on a map or globe.

Musicians with a Message

Academic Track: Art/Music

Academic Pathways: Lesson A: Taking notes
Understanding idiomatic language
Lesson B: Reading interviews and profiles
Lesson C: Presenting one main idea in a paragraph
Writing sentences to explain a preference

Unit Theme

Often a musician's goal in performing is simply to provide entertainment, but some musicians also want to send a message to bring about social awareness and change.

Unit 8 explores the topic of musicians with a message as it relates to:

– benefit concerts to raise awareness
– a band from the Democratic Republic of the Congo
– the WOMAD festival of world music
– three musicians making a difference

Think and Discuss *(page 141)*

5 mins

- Ask students to look at the photo and read the caption. What does being a "blues" musician mean? (Answer: Blues is a genre, or type, of music that started about a century ago along the Mississippi River. Typically, blues musicians were poor black men who sang about their life experiences. The style was popularized by musicians like B.B. King.) Ask if students know about Keb' Mo or other blues singers. (He's a musician who writes songs and sings, accompanying himself on the guitar.)

- For question 1 ask students about their favorite musicians. Make a list on the board, and note whether musicians are solo performers or members of a group. Do they write their own music and lyrics, or do they perform songs written by other songwriters? What are the topics of some of the students' favorite songs?

- Discuss question 2. Lead a class discussion on how musicians can change the world. The Playing for Change movement aims to promote peace by bringing together people from different backgrounds through music. Sometimes musicians from around the world collaborate on a single piece of music. Click on the video at http:// playingforchange.com/ for an example.

Exploring the Theme

15 mins

(pages 142–143)

The photo shows Bono performing. He and his band, U2, have been pioneers in dealing with social issues.

- Ask: *What's a benefit concert?* (Answer: It's a performance to raise money and awareness for a humanitarian cause.) Ask volunteers to summarize the causes or beneficiaries behind each of the events. (Answers: The Concert for Bangladesh: refugees from what was then East Pakistan; Live Aid: famine in Ethiopia; Live 8: poor people; Live Earth: climate change; Playing for Change: peace.)

- Discuss the three questions on page 142.

Answer Key

Possible answers:
1. Answers will vary.
2. Famous musicians attract their fans to benefit concerts. Many stars have a social conscience that motivates them to participate in such events.
3. This is an ongoing project, not something focused on concerts on one particular date.

TIP   Ask students if there is a local cause that a benefit concert could help. What is it? Benefit concerts don't always need to have famous performers. Could popular local performers help to promote this cause?

Preparing to Read *(page 144)*

30 mins

WARM-UP

The Lesson A target vocabulary is presented in two different exercises: a matching task and a sentence-completion activity.

Exercise A. | Building Vocabulary

- Have students find the blue words in the reading passage and use the other words around them to guess their meanings. Then ask students to work individually to match the sentence parts to make definitions.

- Check the answers as a class by asking volunteers to read out a sentence each.

- Point out the **Word Link** box. *Dis-* is another prefix with the effect of negating the root word. Ask the students about the prefixes they've encountered that mean the same. (Answers: *un-* in Unit 1, *in-* in Unit 2, and *im-/in-*, *un-* in Unit 7)

Vocabulary Notes

Appearance is a key term in the reading passage because its translation is part of the band's name. *Appearance* is the way that someone or something looks, but appearances can often be misleading and give a false impression. For example, some people might see the band Staff Benda Bilili as disabled, but the band members see themselves as rock musicians with a positive message. The expression *"keeping up appearances"* means that someone is trying to look as though things are going well when in fact they are not.

Answer Key

1. d 2. c 3. a 4. e 5. b

Exercise B. | Building Vocabulary

- After students locate the words in the passage and guess their meaning from context, have them work individually to complete the sentences.

- Check answers as a class.

Answer Key

1. instrument 2. encourage 3. perform 4. founder
5. energetic

Exercise C. | Using Vocabulary

- Students apply the new vocabulary items by answering questions in which these words are the most significant terms.

- After completing their answers individually, have students compare answers in pairs.

- Ask volunteers to share their ideas and opinions with the class.

Answer Key

Possible answers:
1. Many classical composers—such as Bach or Mozart—are well known, but in the case of popular music, the person who performs a song and makes it a hit is often better known than the composer.
2. Answers will vary.

TIP Ask students about bands that perform in their area. What kind of music do they play? Do local bands ever give benefit concerts? If so, what issue are they trying to make people aware of?

Exercise D. | Brainstorming

- By now, students know that brainstorming is a way to come up with a lot of ideas in very little time. In this case, the word web is a graphic organizer that shows how ideas are related to why music is important.

- After students fill in the word web, have the class work together to share ideas. Draw a word web on the board, and fill it in with students' ideas.

Answer Key

Possible answers:
inspires people, relaxes people, is exciting, brings people together, helps people express their thoughts and feelings

Exercise E. | Predicting

- Ask students to read the title, subheads, and first paragraph to determine the main idea of the passage.

- Note: Students will check their predictions later, in exercise **A** on page 147.

track **2-07**

Ask students to read the passage. Explain that the vocabulary definitions in the footnotes at the bottom of pages 145 and 146 will help them understand the reading.

Overview of the Reading

The passage describes a group of Congolese street musicians who are disabled but overcome their problems through music. The group's goal is to communicate the message that you can be positive and strong even when life is difficult. The band conveys the message in many ways: through their lyrics, in their performances, in their inclusion of street children in their work, and—most important—by seeing themselves as capable rock musicians. Although the group's home base is the streets of Kinshasa, a French film crew made a documentary about them and they have now made several recordings. In 2009, Staff Benda Bilili won the Artist Award at WOMEX (World Music Expo).

IDEAS FOR... Expansion

The passage describes the members of Staff Benda Bilili as *disabled*, but some TV video captions use the word *handicapped* or *crippled*. These latter two words have a negative connotation, and in some countries people with disabilities say that the words are disrespectful. Four of the band's members had polio when they were younger, and the disease left them with limited mobility. This is one of the reasons that they get around on the special tricycles shown on pages 145 and 150. On stage—as shown in the photo on page 146—they use wheelchairs and crutches. One of the main points Staff Benda Bilili want to emphasize is that they should be judged by the music they make and the lives they lead, not by their disabilities. Have students watch the video at http://www.youtube.com/watch?v=KzCUcO_d1qI to see how the group functions as they promote vaccinations for polio.

Understanding the Reading
(page 147)

45 mins

Exercise A. | Understanding the Gist

Check students' predictions in exercise **E** on page 144. Did they guess the general idea correctly?

Answer Key

The correct answer is b. The passage discusses the band called Staff Benda Bilili, a group made up of disabled musicians—not a benefit concert.

Exercise B. | Understanding the Main Ideas

- Allow time for students to work individually or in pairs to identify the main idea of each of the two sections of the passage.

- Check the answers as a class. Ask volunteers to say why the other two options are not correct. (Answer: The incorrect options express a supporting detail—not the main idea.)

Answer Key

1. b 2. a

Exercise C. | Identifying Key Details

- Tell students to use the reading passage to decide if the information is true (T) or false (F).
- Have students complete the task individually and then compare answers in pairs. Remind the class to correct the false statements.
- Check answers as a class.

Answer Key

1. F (Roger, the guitar player, is not physically disabled.)
2. F (It means "look beyond appearances.")
3. T
4. F (He gets out of his wheelchair to dance on his hands.)
5. T
6. T

Exercise D. | Critical Thinking: Evaluating Attitude

- Have students read the **CT Focus** box carefully, recalling that an idiom is a set phrase that has a different meaning from the individual words by themselves.
- Have students discuss the questions in pairs. Encourage them to write new idioms in their vocabulary notebook.
- Ask for volunteers to share their answers with the class.

Answer Key

Possible answers:
1. When people look at the band, they see men with disabilities. However, the physical challenges do not limit what the men are able to do as musicians.
2. It's easy for disadvantaged people to wait for someone else to come to their aid, but these men have made their own opportunities and encourage others to do the same.
3. Answers will vary.

45 mins

Developing Reading Skills
(page 148)

Reading Skill: Taking Notes

- Go over the information in the box. Draw students' attention to the **Strategy** box. Stress that notes should consist of only key points and should be written in "shorthand," using phrases and not complete sentences. Point out how paraphrasing, or using readers' own words, helps them to remember the material better.

- Direct students to the helpful list on the top of page 211, and go over any abbreviations that need further explanation.

- Explain that graphic organizers such as Venn diagrams, idea webs, or time lines can help students organize content when taking notes.

> **TIP** One way of making the point about taking *brief* notes is to have students use highlighters and mark no more than three words in the passage for each answer.

Exercise A. | Taking Notes

- Allow time for students to work individually to complete the chart.

- Ask students to compare answers in pairs.

- Point out exercise **B**, where students will use their notes to answer questions about Staff Benda Bilili.

Answer Key

Paragraph B: satongé
Paragraph C: look beyond appearances, Staff Benda Bilili, poor street people
Paragraph E: rock musicians, jumps out of wheelchair, dances on hands
Paragraph F: Kinshasa & rest of D. R. Congo
Paragraph G: song, living with polio, vaccinations

> **TIP** Students need support when they first start taking notes because the tendency is to write too much. As long as notes make sense to the writer, that's enough. Have students read their notes to a partner to prove this point.

Exercise B. | Analyzing

- Tell students to work individually to answer the questions using their notes.

- Check the answers as a class.

Answer Key

1. Their mission is to tell people to be positive and strong.
2. They don't see themselves as disabled. They see themselves as rock musicians.
3. The movie shows how music helped the group survive in a very difficult environment.
4. They get ideas from their problems.

IDEAS FOR... **Expansion**

As a teacher, if you want more background on Staff Benda Bilili, read an interview in http://www.guardian.co.uk/music/2009/nov/01/staff-benda-bilili-congo-interview

Viewing: World Music
(page 149)

Overview of the Video

For 30 years, WOMAD (World of Music, Arts, and Dance) festivals have brought performers from around the world to share their traditional music and dances. The video starts with comments by British rocker Peter Gabriel who is a founder of the festival. He talks about the importance of people being open-minded as they experience arts from other places. The rest of the video focuses on an Italian group named for a street in Naples. The spokesperson says that the music is a combination of folk rock and two traditional dances, but that it is a lot like rap.

Although WOMAD was first organized in Britain, it is now a worldwide music festival. It has remained true to its aims of using a wide range of music, arts, and dance as a way of bridging boundaries between cultures and bringing people together. In addition to performances, there are workshops for adults and children, sampling of foods cooked by the musicians, and a global market where attendees can purchase items from different countries. See the WOMAD website for more details at http://womad.org/

Before Viewing

Exercise A. | Using a Dictionary

- Have students complete the exercise individually.
- Check answers as a class.
- Ask for volunteers to use each of the words in a new sentence.

Answer Key

1. stunning **2.** fan **3.** traditional **4.** open-minded

Exercise B. | Brainstorming

- Students work in pairs to make lists of types of music that are often combined to create a new kind of sound.
- After a while, open the discussion up to the whole class and ask for examples. You might offer the example of Staff Benda Bilili's music, which is a combination of rumba (a dance), reggae, and rhythm 'n' blues. Other examples are fusion jazz, which combines rock + jazz, and country blues, which combines country music + the blues.

While Viewing

Exercises A.

- Ask students to read the questions in exercise **A** so they are prepared to watch and listen for certain information.
- Play the video. Ask students to circle their answers as they watch.
- Point out that students will discuss the statements during the next exercise.
- If necessary, play the video again.

Answer Key

1. T
2. F (Spaccanapoli plays traditional music from Italy.)
3. F (Marcello Collasurdo says the group's music is like rap.)
4. T

After Viewing

Exercise A.

- Have students discuss and compare their answers in pairs. Encourage them to correct the false statements.
- If necessary, play the video again and go over the answers.

Exercise B. | Synthesizing

- Students work in pairs to discuss the questions.
- Walk around the room as students work, providing assistance as necessary.
- When the pairs finish, lead a brief class discussion.

> **TIP** Venn diagrams are useful graphic organizers for comparing and contrasting. Draw a two-circle diagram and suggest that pairs use it to make brief notes as they answer the questions.

Answer Key

Possible answers:
1. Both groups get their inspiration from daily life. However, Staff Benda Bilili wants to send a message to people about taking charge of their lives in a positive way, while Spaccanapoli is more interested in preserving the folk music tradition of Naples, Italy.
2. Both WOMAD and the benefit concerts include a variety of artists and occur in multiple places. WOMAD is primarily about bringing traditional world music to new audiences, whereas the benefit concerts are mostly about raising money for humanitarian causes.

Preparing to Read

(pages 150–151)

30 mins

WARM-UP

The Lesson B target vocabulary is introduced in two activities: in the first one, students are given definitions and then asked to complete sentences using the target words; in the second exercise, they match parts of sentences to make definitions.

Exercise A. | Building Vocabulary

- Ask students to read the definitions in the box and then work individually to choose the correct words to complete the sentences.
- Check the answers as a class.

Answer Key

1. regularly 2. issue 3. improve 4. escape 5. Medicine

Exercise B. | Building Vocabulary

- Allow time for students to find the words in the reading, try to guess their meanings from context, and match the sentence parts.
- Have students compare answers in pairs before you check the answers as a class.

Answer Key

1. d 2. a 3. e 4. b 5. c

Exercise C. | Using Vocabulary

- Draw students' attention to the **Word Partners** box. Ask volunteers to come up with sentences using some of the new expressions. Remind students to write the word partners in their vocabulary notebooks.
- Have students write their answers to the questions individually. Remind them to write complete sentences.
- While students work in pairs to share their ideas, circulate through the classroom listening unobtrusively to students' interactions. Make sure that both partners are participating equally.
- Ask volunteers to share their sentences with the class.

Exercise D. | Scanning

- Have students work individually to scan for the information needed to complete the chart.
- Tell students you will go over the answers later, in exercise **A** on page 154.

track 2-08 Ask students to read the article. Explain that the vocabulary definitions in the footnotes at the bottom of pages 152 and 153 will help them understand the reading.

Overview of the Reading

The reading passage presents profiles of three musicians who are using music to bring attention to some humanitarian issues.

In Unit 7, readers encountered primatologist Mireya Mayor and learned that she was an Emerging Explorer at National Geographic. Given her expeditions in Africa and Madagascar, this was not unusual. Students may be surprised, however, to learn that Zinhle Thabethe is also on the Emerging Explorer list––for her humanitarian work through music. For more information, visit **http://www.nationalgeographic.com/explorers/bios/thabethe-zinhle/**

Understanding the Reading

(page 154)

45 mins

Exercise A. | Understanding the Gist

- Check students' predictions in exercise **D** on page 151.

Answer Key

1. c, Jason Mraz, American
2. a, Zinhle Thabethe, South African
3. b, Arn Chorn-Pond, Cambodian

Exercise B. | Identifying Main Ideas

- Allow time for students to work individually to match each of the four main ideas to the paragraph where it is stated.
- Check answers as a class.

Answer Key

1. F 2. I 3. H 4. E

Exercise C. | Taking Notes

- Explain to students that this activity gives them more practice with taking notes.
- Allow students time to work individually. Encourage them to use as few words as possible in their notes.
- Compare the answers as a class.

Answer Key

Possible answers:
Paragraph E: they can work/make a living, what he saw
Paragraph F: 2002, clinic
Paragraph H: prison camp guards
Paragraph I: Cambodia, young Cambodians

TIP Encourage students to use abbreviations in their notes. To raise awareness of abbreviations, ask students to circle those printed in the notes. They include FTS for Free the Slaves, w/ for *with*, C-P for Chorn-Pond's name, and trad. for *traditional*.

Exercise D. | Using Your Notes

- Have students work in pairs to discuss the questions. Encourage them to refer back to their notes in exercise **C**.

- In order to understand one of the causes of child slavery, students need to make a connection between the last sentence of Paragraph C and the third sentence of Paragraph E. Sometimes parents who are very poor cannot support their children and sell them to traffickers, who buy them and then resell them as slaves. This is illegal, but it happens in some parts of the world. In other places, poor children live alone on the streets, earning a living however they can. Staff Benda Bilili tries to help street kids, and now some of them play percussion in the band.

- After students discuss the questions, open the discussion to the class.

Answer Key

1. Kofi Anan helps parents earn money so they won't have to sell their children.
2. All members of the choir have AIDS, so other people with the disease can relate to them.
3. When he played music, he could escape the prison camp in his mind.

Exercise E. | Critical Thinking: Making Inferences

Have students think about their answers individually. Then lead a class discussion about the questions.

Answer Key

Possible answers:
In the Thabethe quote, "walk the journey" means to live through the course of the disease of an HIV-positive person. Listeners with the disease know that members of Sinikithemba Choir understand what they are going through because they are going through it themselves.

Exercise F. | Critical Thinking: Evaluating

- Have students work in small groups to discuss the issues in the unit.

- As students talk, walk around the class and provide assistance as needed. Make sure students are supporting their opinions with reasons or examples. Some things students might want to take into account are: How many lives will this program save? How will this improve the quality of people's lives? How will this continue to keep a culture alive?

IDEAS FOR... Expansion

Jason Mraz's cause:
Students may want to learn more about child trafficking and what is being done to stop it by UNICEF and other organizations. A Web search will provide this information as well as identify countries where this is an issue.

Arn Chorn-Pond's story:
Chorn-Pond knows what it's like to come to the U.S. knowing only a few words of English and to try to adjust in an American high school. Learn more about his experience at http://www.youtube.com/watch?v=9uHeCzSM_PI

Exploring Written English
(pages 155–157)

45 mins

In this lesson, students go through the process of writing sentences about their favorite musician. The lesson starts with a presentation of language for connecting reasons, or causes, with results and then follows the steps in the writing process. In the final sentences, the students write about why someone or some group is their favorite musician.

Exercise A. | Language for Writing

- Go over the information in the box.
- Have students complete the exercise individually and then compare answers in pairs. Encourage the class to use pronouns to avoid repetition.
- Check the answers as a class.

Answer Key

1. Result: Jason Mraz has traveled around the world playing music. Therefore, he has met a lot of people from different cultures./He has therefore met a lot of people from different cultures.
2. Reason: Since it is very peaceful and relaxing, I listen to classical music before I go to sleep./I listen to classical music before I go to sleep since it is very peaceful and relaxing.
3. Reason: Since music helped Arn Chorn-Pond survive as a child, he wants to use it to help other children./Arn Chorn-Pond wants to use music to help other children since it helped him survive as a child.
4. Result: Peter Gabriel loves world music. Therefore, he decided to start a world music festival./He therefore decided to start a world music festival.

Exercise B.

- Ask students to create two sets of sentences about the situations in which they listen to music. Tell them to use *therefore* in the first two and *since* in the second two.
- Ask volunteers to read out their sentences.

Answer Key

Answers will vary.

Writing Skill: Presenting One Main Idea in a Paragraph

Students are probably aware that a paragraph has one main idea and several supporting details such as examples or reasons. Good writers strive for coherent paragraphs where all the sentences are clearly and logically connected. Some student writers add sentences that are not directly related to the main point of the paragraph, however. This is particularly likely to happen when teachers set an expected "word count" for writing, so students are tempted to pad their work. The following two exercises give students a chance to identify and omit sentences that are not directly related to the main idea of a paragraph.

Exercise C.

- Allow time for students to identify the sentences that are off topic. Have them work individually and then compare answers in pairs.
- Check the answers as a class.

Answer Key

The conductor Adrian Boult also studied at Oxford University.
The film *Man on Wire* won the Academy Award for Best Documentary in 2009.

Exercise D.

- Students work individually to identify and cross out the three sentences that do not pertain to the topic of a musical group from Thailand.
- Check answers as a class.

Answer Key

The population of Thailand is about 70 million.
Before 1939, Thailand was called "Siam."
I think people should visit Thailand, as it is a very interesting country.

Writing Task: Drafting

(page 158)

Exercise A. | Brainstorming

- Ask students to work with a partner to quickly write a list of favorite musicians, bands, and songs—and reasons they like them.
- Monitor students as they work, and help them with ideas if needed.

Exercise B. | Brainstorming

- Go over the steps. Remind students that complete sentences are not necessary at this stage and that it is more important to focus on their ideas than on grammar or spelling.
- Walk around and monitor students as they work. Provide assistance as needed.
- Ask three or four volunteers to share with the class their topic, their three reasons, and their details about each reason.
- You may want to model how this works, using your own favorite musician or group. For example, you could use Bono and the band, U2. Reason 1: like the sound of their music with good tunes and interesting instruments. Reason 2: Bono writes own lyrics, about important social issues. Reason 3: He's an activist, not afraid to speak out, raises money for causes, won TED prize for work to change world, given knighthood by the Queen of England.

Exercise C. | Draft 1

As students write their sentences, walk around and offer help if asked. Refrain from any type of error correction at this point.

Writing Task: Revising and Editing *(page 159)*

Exercise D. | Peer Evaluation

- Go over the three steps with the class.
- Have students use the steps to help them read their partner's work. Point out the emphasis on logical connections with linking words or phrases.
- Make sure that both members of the pair have equal time to give feedback.

Exercise E. | Draft 2

- Walk around and monitor students as they work. Provide assistance as needed.
- Remind students to use the feedback they got from their partner.

Exercise F. | Editing Practice

- Go over the information in the box.
- Allow time for students to work individually to find and correct the errors.
- Go over the answers as a class by writing the sentences on the board and asking volunteers to correct them and explain the errors.

Answer Key

1. **Since** he played music in the camps, Chorn-Pond survived in a difficult situation.
2. Since he wanted to help keep traditional Cambodian music alive, Chorn-Pond went back to Cambodia to teach music.
3. Because music is important in Naples, people there often sing in the streets.
4. Celine Dion was born in Canada. Therefore, some of her songs are in French.
5. Because their instruments are homemade, Staff Benda Bilili's music has a special sound.
6. **Since** Marcello Collasurdo's father played the tambourine, Marcello wanted to learn how to play it, too./Marcello Collasurdo's father played the tambourine. Therefore, Marcello wanted to play it, too./Marcello therefore wanted to play it, too.

Writing Task: Editing *(page 160)*

Exercise G. | Editing Checklist

- Go over the sentences in the editing checklist.
- Allow time for students to read and edit their work.

Exercise H. | Final Draft

Have students complete their final draft, and then collect their work.

Unit Quiz

- Students can work in groups to answer the questions.
- Encourage students to refer back to the relevant pages of the unit to find the answers.
- To do the quiz as a competition, you can have students work in teams.

Answer Key

1. Benefit
2. founder
3. appearances
4. Taking notes
5. responsibilities
6. poor children
7. flute
8. result

IDEAS FOR... **Further Discussion**

Ask students if they keep up with music developments in their own country. One way to catch up is to listen to groups at **http://worldmusic. nationalgeographic.com/** This might be a fun homework assignment. At the start of the next class, find out what students heard.

Behavior

Academic Track: Life Science/Anthropology

Academic Pathways: **Lesson A:** Recognizing noun clauses
                                 Making inferences from an interview
                      Lesson B: Reading news articles about science
                      Lesson C: Writing a topic sentence
                                 Writing a paragraph to compare animals

Unit Theme

Animal behavior fascinates humans, partly because some animals are pets that live in close companionship with people, while other animals—especially nonhuman primates—that live in the wild or in captivity share much of the same genetic heritage with us.

Unit 9 explores the topic of animal behavior as it relates to:

– shared skills of chimpanzees and humans
– the work of a dog trainer
– the ability of gorillas to make tools
– research on monkey behavior

Think and Discuss *(page 161)*

5 mins

- Ask students to describe what they see in the photograph. (Answer: a baby orangutan kissing its mother's face) Is this learned or *instinctive* (inborn) behavior? Orangutans are great apes like gorillas and chimpanzees, but they live only in the rain forests of Indonesia and Malaysia. Babies stay with their mothers for the first two years of life, then go off on their own. Scientists have conducted studies with orangutans and consider them very intelligent. Today, these apes are endangered due to habitat destruction and trapping. For more information, see http://animals.nationalgeographic.com/animals/mammals/orangutan.html

- Discuss question 1 as a class. To some extent, answers will depend on where students live. In most places, there is a distinction between pets and work or farm animals.

- Discuss question 2. Ask volunteers to share their opinions. Not many years ago, scientists thought that humans could do many things other animals couldn't, but now spoken language and communicating about abstract ideas and the future are the main hallmarks. By contrast, animals have a number of innate abilities that humans lack. For instance, migrating birds and butterflies successfully travel long distances with internal navigation systems.

Exploring the Theme *(pages 162–163)*

15 mins

The opening spread has a photograph of a chimpanzee that is using a stick to take off a man's cap.

Ask students to quickly skim the title and two paragraphs on page 163. How do the two paragraphs relate to the title? (Answer: The first paragraph talks about biological closeness between humans and nonhuman primates, while the second discusses the close relationship between humans and dogs.)

Answer Key

Possible answers:

1. Chimpanzees use sounds and gestures to communicate. They can climb trees and use tools.
2. Dogs have a superior sense of smell that is useful in police and rescue work. They can be trained to help people with disabilities such as blindness.
3. Gorillas and orangutans are close to humans in their genetics. Cats live with people as pets. Horses are intelligent animals that are important for transportation in some parts of the world.

IDEAS FOR... Expansion

Interested students can find out more about breeds of dogs and dog behavior at http://ngm.nationalgeographic.com/2002/01/dogs/phillips-text

30 mins

Preparing to Read *(page 164)*

WARM-UP

The Lesson A target vocabulary is introduced through a matching exercise and a sentence-completion task.

Exercise A. | Building Vocabulary

- Have students work individually or in pairs to find the blue words in the reading passage and use the other words around them to guess their meanings. Then have students match the sentence parts to make definitions.
- Check the answers as a class by asking volunteers to read out a sentence each.
- Point out the **Word Usage** box. Ask volunteers to suggest a sentence for each of the uses of *approach*.

Answer Key

1. d 2. c 3. a 4. e 5. b

Exercise B. | Building Vocabulary

- Have students work individually to locate the words in the passage, guess their meanings from context, and use them to complete the sentences.
- Check the answers as a class.

Vocabulary Note

A *professional* is someone who works in a field requiring specialized knowledge and training such as law or medicine. However, *professional* is also used in sports for people who get paid to play instead of doing it for fun or as a pastime. So, a *professional golfer* gets paid, but an amateur golfer doesn't.

Answer Key

1. trainer 2. professional 3. angry 4. integrity
5. powerful

Exercise C. | Using Vocabulary

- Students apply the new vocabulary items by answering questions in which the new words are the key terms.
- After students complete their answers individually, have students work with a partner to take turns reading their sentences aloud.
- Ask volunteers to share their ideas with the class.

Answer Key

Answers will vary.

Exercise D. | Skimming/Predicting

- Have students work individually or in pairs to skim the reading and decide on the topic or topics mentioned in the text.
- Note: Students will check their predictions later, in exercise **A** on page 167.

track 2-09 Ask students to read the passage. Explain that the vocabulary definitions in the footnotes at the bottom of pages 165 and 166 will help them understand the reading.

Overview of the Reading

The passage is an interview with dog trainer Cesar Millan, who has a TV show called *Dog Whisperer*. Millan says that people choose certain types of dogs that reflect their own personalities. He believes that dogs don't think; they obey commands. He also thinks that dog owners have to treat their pets as pets—not as humans. Millan claims that it is humans that must be trained to control and dominate their dogs. In several questions about his family, he says that his father doesn't understand his work and is disappointed that he didn't become a professional.

> **IDEAS FOR...** **Expansion**
>
> From time to time, people claim to have an unusual ability to relate to certain animals. For example, *The Horse Whisperer* (a popular book made into a film) tells the story of a man with a special talent to communicate with horses.

45 mins

Understanding the Reading *(page 167)*

Exercise A. | Understanding the Gist

Check students' predictions in exercise **D** on page 164. Did they guess the topics correctly?

Answer Key

All the topics should be checked except for: how and why Millan became a dog trainer what a normal day is like for Millan.

Exercise B. | Identifying Key Details

- Allow time for students to work individually to complete the sentences with information from the interview.
- Check answers as a class.

Answer Key

1. humanizing
2. feminine
3. powerful, can't control
4. walk their dogs
5. to live in the moment, honesty and integrity

Vocabulary Note

Note the use of *issues* in line 27 to mean "problems."

Exercise C. | Critical Thinking: Making Inferences

- Have students read the **Strategy** box carefully. Go over the information with the class, noting that an inference is an idea that is implied but not directly stated. Explain that making inferences is "reading between the lines," that is, using what is said to understand attitudes and opinions.

- Point out that the task has two steps: identifying who Millan is talking about and then matching direct statements with inferences. Have students complete the task individually before you check the answers as a class.

- In the interview, Millan uses informal language with idioms. If necessary, explain to students that *stab someone in the back* does not mean literally to knife them, but figuratively to unfairly and secretly hurt someone who trusts you.

Answer Key

1. his clients 2. his parents 3. dogs

a. 2 b. 1 c. 3

Exercise D. | Critical Thinking: Making Inferences

- Allow time for students to discuss the questions in small groups.
- Ask for volunteers to share their ideas.

Answer Key

Possible answers:
1. Millan seems to judge people by appearances. He thinks he can tell about the owner's personality by the breed of dog he or she has. (The photographs on page 166 exemplify this because the tough pit bull is shown in a truck in the country, while the poodle seems to have an affluent urban woman owner.)
2. Millan understands that Mexican culture values machismo, an exaggerated idea of manliness that doesn't permit men to tell women that they appreciate and love them. Millan views this attitude in a negative way.

⦿ Developing Reading Skills

45 mins *(page 168)*

Reading Skill: Recognizing Noun Clauses

- Go over the information in the box.

- Refer students to the coverage in the Independent Student Handbook on page 217. It presents three types of noun clauses: those that start with *wh-* words, those using *if* or *whether*, and those starting with *that*. The text box on page 168 focuses on noun clauses starting with *wh-* words. However, exercise **C** uses all three kinds, so it is helpful to go over page 217 with the class before they do exercise **C**.

Exercise A. | Identifying Noun Clauses

- This skill focus gives students practice in identifying *wh-* noun clauses. Point out that in each of these sentences, the clause is an object.

- Have students work individually to identify and underline the noun clause in each sentence.

- Check answers as a class by having volunteers each write a clause on the board.

Answer Key

1. what dogs need
2. why pet owners have trouble with their dogs
3. how to control their dogs
4. how many dog owners there are in the United States
5. where most pet owners get their dogs

Exercise B. | Matching

- Have students work individually to match noun clauses to complete sentences as they're written in the reading. Reference to the passage is important because some of the options in the right-hand column can logically be used for more than one sentence.

- Check the answers as a class.

Answer Key

1. c 2. d 3. a 4. b

track 2-10

Exercise C. | Applying

- Have students work alone to underline the noun clauses in the paragraph. Note that in the first sentence, there is a clause within another noun clause.

- After students compare answers in pairs and correct them as necessary, allow time for them to discuss the questions.

Answer Key

Some people think <u>that your preference for dogs or cats says a lot</u> about <u>who you are</u>. Sam Gosling, a psychologist at the University of Texas in Austin, decided to find out <u>if this is true</u>. In particular, Gosling wanted to learn <u>what the characteristics of certain types of pet owners are</u>. In the study, Gosling first found out <u>how people classify themselves: as dog people, cat people, neither, or both</u>. Then he gave the same people a standard personality test. The results showed <u>what Gosling expected: dog people and cat people are different</u>. For example, Gosling learned <u>that dog people are more outgoing than cat people, and cat people are generally more imaginative than dog people</u>. <u>Why these differences exist</u>, however, is still a mystery.

Answer Key

1. He wanted to know if a preference for dogs or cats reflects a person's personality.
2. First, he found out how people classify themselves.
3. Dog people are more outgoing but less imaginative than cat people.

Viewing: Gorilla Toolmakers *(page 169)*

30 mins

Overview of the Video

Field researchers Thomas Breuer and Emma Stokes discovered that gorillas in northern Congo could think through problems and create tools to solve them.

Primatologists were aware that chimpanzees made and used tools, but until this research, they did not realize that gorillas living in the wild did, too. The researchers managed to get photographs of gorillas using tools, the first time this had been documented.

As Emma Stokes says in the video, long-term observation of animals in their natural habitat is very important. Even then, however, you cannot observe everything that animals do.

Anthropologist Louis Leakey was the first major supporter of long-term primate observation, backing Jane Goodall's years of observing chimpanzees, Dian Fossey's work with mountain gorillas, as well as Birute Galdikas' work with orangutans. As more of the natural habitat diminishes for these primates, time is running out for researchers to observe them in the wild.

To learn more about the research on gorilla tool use behind this video, visit **http://news.nationalgeographic. com/news/2005/09/0930_050930_gorilla_tool.html**

Before Viewing

Exercise A. | Using a Dictionary

- Tell students they will become familiar with some of the key vocabulary in the video by looking up the words in the box and completing the definitions.
- Allow time for students to complete the task.
- Compare the answers as a class.
- Ask for volunteers to use each of the words and phrases in a new sentence.

Vocabulary Note

When you *invent* something, you create a thing that didn't exist before. In this case, two separate female gorillas used sticks in a new way to solve a problem. By contrast, when you *discover* something, you become aware of something that was not known before, such as the mouse lemur discussed in the Unit 7 video.

Answer Key

1. measure the depth of
2. think through
3. invent
4. Evidence

Exercise B. | Brainstorming

Ask pairs of students to talk about what people can do that gorillas cannot. Many differences are apparent, but remind the class that gorillas can express emotions such as happiness or grief, can develop strong friendships and family ties, and can deal with abstract thought. Some, such as Koko, who lived in a laboratory, have even learned a form of human sign language.

While Viewing

Exercise A

- Ask students to read the beginnings and endings of the sentences in exercise **A** so they are prepared to watch and listen for certain information.
- Play the video. Ask students to check their answers in exercise **B** in Before Viewing and to match the two parts of the sentences according to what they see and hear.
- If necessary, play the video again, pausing it at each relevant item.
- Tell students they will check and discuss their answers during the next exercise.

After Viewing

Exercise A.

- Have students discuss and compare answers.
- If necessary, watch the video again and check answers.

Answer Key

1. c 2. e 3. a 4. b 5. d

Exercise B. | Synthesizing

Put students into pairs or small groups to compare dog and gorilla behavior, and then contrast these two animals' behavior with human behavior.

Answer Key

Possible answers:
Both dogs and gorillas exhibit a good deal of innate behavior. For example, some dogs are bred to herd other animals. They have an instinct for how to do this and do not need to be taught. However, dogs are domesticated animals and have coexisted with people for thousands of years, whereas all gorillas—even those in captivity—are wild animals.

30 mins

Preparing to Read
(pages 170–171)

WARM-UP

The Lesson B target vocabulary is introduced in two activities asking students to first guess meaning from context and then complete a matching exercise and a sentence-completion task.

Exercise A. | Building Vocabulary

- Explain the task: Students encounter vocabulary words highlighted in blue within the context of a paragraph; they are to match sentence parts to create appropriate definitions.
- Allow time for students to work individually and then compare answers in pairs.
- Check the answers as a class.

Answer Key

1. d **2.** c **3.** e **4.** a **5.** b

Exercise B. | Building Vocabulary

- Draw students' attention to the **Word Partners** box, which points out that *research* can be used as an adjective (as in *research findings*) or as a noun (e.g., *recent research*).
- After students complete the exercise individually, check the answers as a class.
- Remind students to add these new phrases to their vocabulary notebooks.

Answer Key

1. fair **2.** field **3.** continue **4.** Cooperation **5.** research

---

IDEAS FOR... **Expansion**

In most academic fields or subjects, students have to do some research. In classes at your institution, what does such research entail? What sources are students expected to use? How are they supposed to document their sources? To what extent do students rely on secondary sources or original research? The latter can include things like experiments, surveys, and interviews. Discuss this with the class.

Exercise C. | Using Vocabulary

- Draw students' attention to the next **Word Partners** box, about common collocations with the word *field*. When people do *field research*, they often write up *field notes*. In this unit's video, you see Thomas Breuer using his laptop computer to make *field notes* about his observations.
- Have students answer the questions individually. Remind students to respond to the questions with complete sentences.
- While students share their sentences with a partner, circulate through the classroom listening unobtrusively to students' interactions. Make sure that both partners are participating equally.

Answer Key

Answers will vary.

Exercise D. | Skimming/Predicting

- Ask students to use the main title and the headings to predict the type of passage they are going to read and to guess the main idea of the text.
- Note: Students will check their answers later, in exercise **A** on page 174.

track 2-11
Ask students to read the article. Explain that the vocabulary definitions in the footnotes at the bottom of page 173 will help them understand the reading.

Overview of the Reading

The reading passage contains two news stories about recent scientific research with primates. In the first article, pairs of capuchin monkeys exchanged a rock with a researcher and got rewards. One of the pair was given a better reward than the other, something that caused a bad reaction from its partner. Scientists are not sure whether fair treatment is a cause or a result of cooperative behavior.

In the second report, macaques were given large doses of oxytocin, a hormone related to bonding and maternal behavior. After the administration of the hormone, the monkey had to choose whether to drink juice, give the juice to another monkey, or neither. Monkeys that had received the hormone were more likely to give the juice away. Scientists wonder if there is an application of their results to autistic people who seldom interact with others. However, scientists caution that more research is necessary before they can use the hormone with humans.

People who want to keep up with science news can easily do so by checking the site http://news.nationalgeographic.com/news/ or the news section of *Scientific American* http://www.scientificamerican.com/section.cfm?id=news

Understanding the Reading
(page 174)

45 mins

Exercise A. | Understanding the Gist

Check students' predictions in exercise **D** on page 171.

Answer Key

b, b

Exercise B. | Identifying Main Ideas

- Ask students to work individually to match main ideas from the first article to the functions of the ideas within the reading passage.
- Check the answers with the class.

Answer Key

1. d 2. b 3. a 4. e 5. c

Exercise C. | Identifying Main Ideas

- Explain that, like the previous exercise, the task is to associate main ideas with their function in the second article. Have students work individually or in pairs to complete the sentences with key ideas.
- Check the answers as a class.

Answer Key

2. oxytocin, another macaque
3. give the juice to another monkey
4. more sociable/kinder
5. autism

Exercise D. | Understanding Pronoun Reference

- Allow time for students to work individually to complete the task and then compare answers in pairs.
- Check the answers as a class.

Answer Key

Monkeys Show a Sense of Fairness
1. a 2. b 3. b

"Love Drug" Results in Kinder Monkeys
1. a 2. b 3. a

> **TIP** Ask students to work in pairs and roleplay TV interviews with the researchers. Assign roles of reporters and researchers. Have the rest of the class be the studio audience. After the interview, let members of the audience ask questions about the studies.

> **IDEAS FOR... Expansion**
>
> There is a great deal of research on nonhuman primates because of their close genetic relationship with people. In the United States, for example, there are eight federally funded primate research centers. Have students search under the keywords *primate research* or visit some of the sites to learn what kind of research is going on in these laboratories.

45 mins

Exploring Written English
(pages 175–177)

In this lesson, students go through the process of writing a paragraph comparing the behavior of two kinds of animals. The lesson starts with a presentation of language for making comparisons and then follows the steps in the writing process.

Exercise A. | Language for Writing: Making Comparisons

- Go over the information in the box.
- Allow time for students to work individually to complete the task and then compare answers in pairs.
- Check the answers as a class.

Answer Key

1. Unlike gorillas, dogs cannot make tools.
2. Both apes and monkeys eat insects.
3. Reptiles lay eggs. In contrast, mammals give birth to live babies.
4. Old World monkeys, such as macaques, live in the Eastern Hemisphere. However, New World monkeys, such as capuchins, live in the Western Hemisphere./New World monkeys, such as capuchins, however, live in the Western Hemisphere.
5. German shepherds can become guide dogs. Similarly, capuchin monkeys can be trained to help people.

> **IDEAS FOR... Geographic Literacy**
>
> After exercise **A**, ask students to name continents and countries in the Eastern Hemisphere. Continents would include Europe, Africa, Asia, and Australia. In contrast, the Western Hemisphere covers North, Central, and South America.

Exercise B.

- Allow time for students to work in pairs to use a Venn diagram to compare and contrast two breeds of dogs. Remind the class that the overlapping area in the center pertains to both types of dogs, while the yellow and blue areas apply to only one type of dog.
- Check the answers as a class by asking volunteers to each write a sentence on the board.

Answer Key

Possible answers:
Similarities: Both Australian terriers and Basenjis are alert, social, and easy to train. Like the Australian terrier, the Basenji is normally good with children.
Differences: Unlike the Australian terrier who can live 14 years, the Basenji usually lives 10 to 12 years. The Australian terrier barks a lot. The Basenji, however, doesn't bark much. The Australian terrier can breed twice a year. In contrast, the Basenji can breed only once a year.

> **IDEAS FOR... Grammar Review**
>
> The Independent Student Handbook on page 218 provides an overview of terms for making comparisons.

Writing Skill: Writing a Topic Sentence

- If necessary, explain to students that in both reading and writing, a topic sentence should clearly express the main point of the paragraph as well as give some hint about how the main idea will be developed or discussed.
- Go over the information in the box.

Exercise C.

- Ask students to work in pairs to choose the most appropriate topic sentence.
- Check the answer as a class.

Answer Key

The best choice is b. The rest of the paragraph describes why Basenjis are easy to train and why they are good with children. Option a is not correct because the paragraph doesn't compare Basenjis with other dogs vis a vis safety. Option c is too general and applies to all kinds of pets.

Exercise D. | Writing a Topic Sentence

- Allow time for students to work individually to write a topic sentence for the paragraph.
- Check the answers as a class by asking volunteers to read out their ideas. Write their sentences on the board, and take a class vote to choose the best ones.

Answer Key

Possible answer:
Gorillas demonstrate their intelligence by making tools and communicating with humans.

Writing Task: Drafting

(page 178)

Exercise A. | Brainstorming

- Ask students to work in pairs to quickly write some ideas about animals and their behavior.
- Walk around the room while students are making their lists. Provide assistance as needed.

Exercise B. | Planning

- At this stage, students again use a Venn diagram—this time to work individually to organize their ideas for comparing the behavior of two animals. Make sure they know how to list details that apply to one of or both of the animals.
- When students finish their notes, have them write a topic sentence that includes the main idea as well as suggestions about other points that will be covered.
- If necessary, model a Venn diagram, using *Cats* as Animal 1 and *Dogs* as Animal 2. In the circle under *Cats*, write: *independent, happy indoors, clean themselves, use a litter box*. In the circle under *Dogs*, write: *need attention and room for exercise, must be washed, need to walk them outdoors several times a day*. Under Both, write: *affectionate, intelligent, live 10 years or longer, eat commercial pet food*. As the topic sentence, write: *Both cats and dogs are common pets, but each has characteristics that make them better suited to some families than others*.

Exercise C. | Draft 1

As students write their paragraphs, walk around and offer help if asked. Refrain from any type of error correction at this point.

Writing Task: Revising and Editing *(page 179)*

Exercise D. | Peer Evaluation

- Go over the steps in the exercise. Point out the emphasis on the topic sentence and the points of comparison.
- Remind students to read mostly for ideas. Suggest that students give some positive feedback to their partner as their first comment.
- Walk around the class as students work, making sure that both members of the pair have equal time to give feedback.

Exercise E. | Draft 2

- Walk around and monitor students as they work. Provide assistance as needed.
- Remind students to use the feedback they got from their partner.

Exercise F. | Editing Practice

- Go over the information in the box.
- Allow time for students to work individually to find and correct the errors.
- Go over the sentences as a class by asking volunteers to read out the correct sentences and explain the errors.

Answer Key

1. Like humans, chimpanzees make tools to solve problems.
2. Both female capuchins and humans **value** fairness.
3. Some chimpanzees make tools in zoos. **In** contrast, gorillas rarely make tools in captivity.
4. Unlike cats, dogs need a lot of attention from their owners.
5. Some dog trainers believe in punishing bad behavior. However**,** other trainers believe in rewarding good behavior.
6. Both a basenji and an Australian terrier **make** good pets for children.
7. Scientists often use monkeys in behavioral studies. Similarly**,** rats are useful in scientific research on behavior.
8. Like children**,** dogs need a lot of training and attention.

Writing Task: Editing

(page 180)

Exercise G. | Editing Checklist

- Go over the sentences in the editing checklist.
- Allow time for students to read and edit their work.
- Ask for some examples of each type of error.

Exercise H. | Final Draft

Have students complete their final draft, and then collect their work.

> **TIP** You can use students' sentences to collect (anonymous) examples of good sentences and common errors for the next class.

Unit Quiz

- Students can work in groups to answer the questions.
- Encourage students to refer back to the relevant pages of the unit to find the answers.
- To do the quiz as a competition, you can have students work in teams.

Answer Key

1. chimpanzee
2. approach to
3. tell you what to do
4. noun
5. tools
6. Cooperation
7. fairness
8. topic sentence

IDEAS FOR... **Expansion**

Item 5 on page 175 mentions capuchin monkeys as helpers for disabled people. This idea is highly controversial. An organization called Monkey Helpers (see http://www.monkeyhelpers.org/) believes that these intelligent animals can assist people with disabilities. However, animal experts including the American Veterinary Association and the ASPCA say that adult capuchins are dangerous and cannot be trusted as assistance animals. Interested students could research both sides of this controversy and then debate it in class.

The Power of Image

Academic Track: Interdisciplinary

Academic Pathways: Lesson A: Recognizing subordinating conjunctions
Understanding mood

Lesson B: Reading a personal narrative

Lesson C: Using supporting ideas in a descriptive paragraph
Writing a paragraph to describe a photograph

Unit Theme

People respond to photographs on many levels: emotional, analytical, experiential. Photographs can arouse our feelings, make us think about issues, and remind us of memories. This unit uses photographs to explore all these dimensions.

Unit 10 explores the topic of photography as it relates to:

– documenting social issues
– artistic qualities of photographs
– a camp for young refugees
– a photographer's encounter with a leopard seal

Think and Discuss (page 181)

5 mins

Ask students to describe the photograph. (Answer: a worried-looking mother with three children) Have students read the caption and say why they think the woman looks the way she does. Remind them of *migrate*, a target vocabulary word presented on page 44. During the Depression, the farming area in the center of the U.S. was affected by dust storms. Many people left and migrated to California where they worked in agriculture. Even there, times were tough and families barely survived. Dorothea Lange's famous photograph captured the sense of worry and despair that the woman was feeling. Students can read about Lange's experience photographing the migrant woman at http://en.wikipedia.org/wiki/Dorothea_Lange

Dorothea Lange was famous for documentary photography, using images to record important historical and social movements. Sometimes she took hundreds of photos on the same topic.

- Discuss question 1 as a class. Ask why some photographs are beautiful, and others affect people emotionally. What qualities do powerful photographs have?

- Discuss question 2. Ask students to describe their favorite photograph. If possible, ask students to bring favorite photos to class.

TIP Be prepared to model the activity to show how to describe a photo. Bring in a photograph and describe it to the class, explaining why you find it a powerful or special image.

Exploring the Theme (pages 182–183)

15 mins

- Read the paragraph at the top of page 183. Have them circle the six key elements highlighted in **bold**.

- For question A1, these are the elements that make a photograph outstanding. For question A2, students can add other ideas.

- For question B, have students work in groups to match the photographs with the important elements. Although some answers may be better than others, make sure students express their own opinions and give reasons for them.

Answer Key

A1. Griffiths identifies composition, moment, light. Other elements are color, motion, wonder.

A2. Possible answers: an emotional quality, something that changes the way we see things.

B. Possible answers: The composition of the mother and her baby and the pink color of the carriage. Capture attention. The photo of the boy and buffaloes captures motion and a "moment" in time. The light of the sea lion photo creates a sense of wonder.

Preparing to Read *(page 184)*

30 mins

WARM-UP

The Lesson A target vocabulary is presented in context, and students are to choose between two options to complete sentences.

Exercise A. | Building Vocabulary

- Have students find the words in the reading and use the other words around them to guess their meanings. Then have them complete the sentences using one of the two words or phrases.

- Check the answers by asking volunteers to each read out a sentence.

- The **Word Link** box focuses on words with the Latin root *vis-*, meaning "to see." This is a good opportunity to review the affixes summarized on page 211. Write the following words on the board, and have students figure out what they mean from their parts: *revise* (to see again), *invisible* (can't be seen), *envision* (to see into something, like the future).

Answer Key

1. illegal	6. adult
2. ceremony	7. points out
3. quality	8. visual
4. suddenly	9. remind you of
5. emotion	10. element

Exercise B. | Using Vocabulary

After students discuss the questions in pairs, ask for volunteers to share their answers with the class.

Answer Key

Answers will vary.

Exercise C. | Brainstorming

- Have students call out words that describe emotions. Write the words on the board. Then go through them as a class, writing an emoticon after each one to indicate positive ☺ or negative ☹.

- Have students work in pairs to brainstorm additional emotion words.

- Ask volunteers to suggest some positive and negative emotions as reactions to the photos on pages 185–188.

Answer Key

Possible answers:
Positive emotions: joy, relief, sympathy, love generosity, delight, fun
Negative emotions: anger, fear, sorrow, hate, shock, shame, envy, embarrassment

Exercise D. | Predicting

- Have students work individually to skim page 185 to find out about David Griffin.

- Note: Students will check their predictions later, in exercise **A** on page 189.

track **2-12**

Ask students to read the passage. The vocabulary definitions in the footnotes at the bottom of pages 185, 187, and 188 will help them understand the reading.

Overview of the Reading

The passage is based on a TED talk given by David Griffin in which he talks about what makes a great picture and how photographers create powerful images. (See link to TED talk on the bottom of page 188.) First, Griffin explains what he means by a "flashbulb memory," when the elements of an event and the viewer's emotions come together in a very clear way. He says the best professional photojournalists use pictures to tell a story so that people become aware of something they hadn't known before. However, he says that amateur photographers can also capture special moments, though perhaps not as often. He closes with a photo he likes because it reminds him of a famous piece of art although it was taken in a remote setting.

> ### IDEAS FOR... Expansion
>
> On the main National Geographic photography site, there is a tab for photographers, including many mentioned in this unit. Clicking on a name will bring up a brief biographical sketch of the person as well as links to his or her photographs. The site also features collections of award-winning photographs. http://photography.nationalgeographic.com/photography/

> ### IDEAS FOR... Expansion
>
> National Geographic's photography page at http://photography.nationalgeographic.com/photography/ is a rich resource with thousands of photographs organized into categories as well as suggestions for taking better pictures.

Understanding the Reading *(page 189)*

45 mins

Exercise A. | Understanding the Gist

Check students' predictions in exercise **D** on page 184. Did they figure out the relationship between Griffin and the other photographers?

Answer Key

Watching the TED talk cited at the bottom of page 188 will help students answer the questions. David Griffin is Director of Photography for National Geographic. What links him to the other photographs is that they are all by National Geographic photographers, and they are photographs that Griffin personally likes and believes are great images. In terms of content, all the photographs capture moments in time to make an emotional connection and tell a story or make people aware of an issue.

Exercise B. | Understanding the Main Ideas

- Have students work individually to answer the questions.
- Before checking the answers as a class, have students compare answers in pairs.

Answer Key

1. A wave almost pulled him out to sea.
2. It's when all the elements of an event come together, including emotions.
3. It works the way the mind does, showing the event (including details), as well as the story and feelings behind it.

Exercise C. | Identifying Key Details

- Have students work individually to match the descriptions to the photographs.
- Check the answers as a class.

Answer Key

1. shark or dead gorilla
2. Mbuti children
3. flying coats
4. celebration in Mumbai slum
5. dead gorilla or shark

Exercise C. | Critical Thinking: Understanding Mood

- Draw students' attention to the **CT Focus** box about mood. Explain that writers sometimes use sensory details to describe what they see, hear, and/or feel to create a particular mood in their writing. Writers can also create a moods by using words that have strong positive or negative associations. Understanding the mood that a writer creates can help you experience the situation the way the writer did.
- Ask students to work in pairs to discuss the questions.
- Lead a brief class discussion to give students the opportunity to share their ideas.

Answer Key

Possible answers:
shock and fear; The incident happened suddenly, yet "time seemed to slow down" so Griffin felt and remembered all the details. His use of the verbs *caught, pull,* and *crash* and the phrase *his face in terror* emphasize the danger of the situation and communicate a mood of fear.

Exercise D. | Critical Thinking: Analyzing

- Allow time for students to discuss the questions with a partner.
- Have volunteers share their ideas with the class.

Answer Key

Possible answers:
1. The story explains the concept of a "flashbulb memory."
2. Yes, because Griffin's description of the moment makes the reader understand exactly how he felt.

Developing Reading Skills *(page 190)*

45 mins

Reading Skill: Recognizing Subordinating Conjunctions

- Go over the information in the box. Point out that *while* appears in both categories, and explain that it is preceded by a comma when used to make a contrast.

- The coverage in the Independent Student Handbook on page 214 lists these linking words by purpose and gives examples of each one.

Exercise A. | Recognizing Subordinating Conjunctions

- Allow time for students to complete the task individually.

- Check the answers as a class.

Answer Key

1. T 2. C 3. T 4. T 5. C

Exercise B. | Scanning/Analyzing

- Have students complete the activity individually and then discuss their answers in pairs.

- Check the answers by asking volunteers to write the sentences on the board, underlining the conjunction in each one and indicating whether it shows contrast or a time relationship.

Answer Key

1. Paragraph A: <u>As</u> Griffin ran to help his son, time seemed to slow down. Time
2. Paragraph E: <u>Although</u> life in the slum is hard, Bendiksen was able to show the spirit and strength of this community. Contrast
3. Paragraph F: <u>As</u> the storm approached, he caught his two daughters throwing their coats into the strong wind. Time
4. Paragraph G: <u>After</u> they saw these photographs, people around the world became more aware of the dangers facing these wild animals. Time

Exercise C. | Applying

Students choose two photographs and write a sentence about each using coordinating conjunctions.

Answer Key

Possible answers:
1. Jane Goodall stayed absolutely still **while** the chimpanzee touched her hair. (Time)
2. **Even though** the picture of the Mbuti children seems scary at first, you realize the feeling is very calm. (Contrast)

Viewing: Photo Camp
(page 191)

Overview of the Video

Professional photographers Reza Deghati, Ed Kashi, Chris Rainier, and Neo Ntsoma worked with 60 young refugees in a camp in Uganda to teach them the basics of photography. They encouraged the refugees to tell their life stories through photos. Although the young people came from different parts of Africa and spoke different languages, they could communicate through photographs.

In the photo camp, the participants learned to use cameras and how to compose pictures. Deghati told them photos are more than just pictures of their friends. Photos can also tell about the good and bad parts of people's lives.

Some youths in the camp developed marketable skills they would be able to use later, but all developed a new way of thinking about their lives. This is evident in the exhibition held at the end of the camp.

National Geographic has sponsored photo camps in various places, bringing young people together to learn to use cameras to document their lives.

To learn more about photo camps, visit **http://photography.nationalgeographic.com/photography/photo-tips/?source=NavPhoTip**

Before Viewing

Exercise A. | Using a Dictionary

- Have students work individually to become familiar with some of the key vocabulary in the video by looking up the words in the box and completing the definitions.
- Check the answers as a class.
- Ask for volunteers to use each of the words in a new sentence.

Answer Key

1. exhibition **2.** portrait **3.** Refugees **4.** reflection
5. document

Exercise B. | Brainstorming

- Have students work in pairs to discuss the question.
- Walk around the room as students talk, providing assistance as needed.
- Ask for volunteers to share their ideas with the class.

Answer Key

Possible answers:
Learning how to take photos is a welcome distraction from their lives in the camp.
Being able to use a camera to tell about their lives will increase the young people's self-esteem.

While Viewing

Exercise A.

- Ask students to read the questions in exercise **A** so they are prepared to watch and listen for certain information.
- Play the video. Ask students to check their answers to the brainstorming exercise in Before Viewing and to circle T or F as they watch.
- If necessary, play the video again.
- Tell students they will check their answers in the next exercise.

After Viewing

Exercise A.

- Have students work in pairs to discuss and compare responses, correcting the false sentences.
- If necessary, watch the video again and check answers.

Answer Key

1. F (The young people in the video have never used cameras before.)
2. T
3. T
4. F (While some students may be inspired to become professional photographers, that is not a goal of the camp.)

Exercise B. | Evaluating

- Have students discuss the question in pairs.
- Lead a brief class discussion about what the photographers learned from the children at the camp.

Answer Key

Possible answers:
They found that some children were talented and that they were motivated to try something new.
They learned how resilient children can be—even in very difficult circumstances.

Preparing to Read

30 mins

(pages 192–193)

WARM-UP

The Lesson B target vocabulary is presented in two sentence-completion exercises: first, students read definitions and then guess meanings from context.

Exercise A. | Building Vocabulary

- Have students work individually to complete the task.

- Check the answers as a class by asking volunteers to each read out a sentence.

Answer Key

1. incredible	4. According to
2. frightened	5. calm
3. disappointed	

Exercise B. | Building Vocabulary

- Have students find the words in the reading and use the other words around them to guess their meanings. Then have students work individually or in pairs to complete the sentences.

- Check the answers as a class.

- Go over the information in the **Word Usage** box. Ask volunteers to come up with a sentence for each of the meanings of the verb *belong*.

Answer Key

1. protect	4. belong to
2. intelligent	5. immediately
3. gear	

IDEAS FOR... **Expansion**

In the bottom photograph on page 195, photographer Nicklen is shown wearing scuba *gear* and using camera *gear* including underwater cameras and special lenses. What gear or equipment is associated with sports the students play? Discuss as a class.

Exercise C. | Using Vocabulary

- Draw students' attention to the next **Word Partners** box about common partners with the verb *protect,* and note that the noun form *protection* is used in question 5.

- Allow time for students to write their sentences individually and then compare ideas in pairs. Remind students to respond to the questions with complete sentences.

- While students are sharing their sentences, circulate through the classroom listening unobtrusively to their interactions. Make sure that both partners are participating equally.

Answer Key

Answers will vary.

Exercise D. | Predicting

- Ask students to work individually to use the pictures and captions to predict what the reading passage is about.

- Note: Students will check their answers later, in exercise **A** on page 196.

track **2-13** Ask students to read the article. Explain that the vocabulary definitions in the footnotes at the bottom of page 195 will help them understand the reading.

Overview of the Reading

The reading passage is a personal narrative (written in the first person singular) of a wildlife photographer's encounter with a dangerous sea animal in Antarctica. Paul Nicklen is experienced in photographing animals in the Arctic but wanted to learn more about leopard seals, huge top predators with a reputation for being fierce hunters. He took an opportunity to dive near an adult female and initially was threatened by her. After a while, the seal stopped her threats and tried to provide Nicklen with live penguins, her typical food. She was puzzled when he didn't respond "properly" according to seal behavior. For four days, she continued her effort to provide food for Nicklen. From this experience, he learned that animals don't always behave in expected ways.

Photographers must be artists, technicians, and often specialists in other fields. Paul Nicklen creates outstanding photographs, masters camera technology (including tricky underwater shots), in addition to being a biologist and an accomplished diver. Even after years of experience in all these areas, he was surprised by his encounter with the leopard seal. To learn more, read his field notes at http://ngm.nationalgeographic.com/2006/11/leopard-seals/nicklen-field-notes or watch a YouTube video about his experience at http://www.youtube.com/watch?v=Zxa6P73Awcg

Understanding the Reading *(page 196)*

Exercise A. | Understanding the Gist

Check students' predictions in exercise **D** on page 193.

Answer Key

Possible answers:
someone's experience with a dangerous sea animal
leopard seal, Paul Nicklen, wildlife photographer, the
Antarctic
He went to Antarctica to find out if leopard seals are
dangerous.
a. a personal narrative

Exercise B. | Identifying Sequence

- Have students work in pairs to sequence the events as they happened in Nicklen's narrative.

- After checking the answers as a class, ask students to take turns telling Nicklen's story in their own words.

Answer Key

From top to bottom: 6, 3, 5, 1, 9, 4, 2, 7, 8

Exercise C. | Critical Thinking: Understanding Mood

- Have students work individually to list words and phrases that describe Nicklen's emotions before and after his experience with the seal.

- Ask students to work with a partner to compare answers.

- Call on volunteers to share their answers with the class.

Answer Key

Possible answers:
Before: frightened, mouth was dry, couldn't even move
After: the most incredible experience, amazing, will stay with me forever

Exercise D. | Critical Thinking: Synthesizing/ Evaluating

- Have students work in small groups to use the elements of good photography from page 183 to analyze three photographs, choosing just three elements for each picture. Encourage students to give reasons for their choices.

- Walk around as students talk, and help them with ideas if needed.

Answer Key

Possible answers:
mouth: 3, 4, 6
carrying penguin: 2, 3, 5
seal and Nicklen: 1, 2, 6

IDEAS FOR... **Expansion**

For more Nicklen photographs, watch his 18-minute TED talk at http://www.ted.com/talks/paul_nicklen_tales_of_ice_bound_wonderlands.html

---

Exploring Written English
(pages 197–199)

45 mins

In this lesson, students go through the process of writing a paragraph describing a photograph and explaining why it is exceptional. The lesson starts with a review of ways to describe spatial relationships and emotions, and then follows the steps in the writing process.

Exercise A. | Analyzing

- Go over the information in the box. Point out that the statements refer to the top photograph on page 183, and the spatial relationships are as seen in the picture—not from the perspective of the participants.

- Explain that some standardized exams, such as the Cambridge PET exam, ask students to describe a picture during the speaking section, so it is important for them to feel comfortable using these terms.

- Allow time for students to work individually to complete the sentences.

- Ask students to compare answers in pairs before checking them as a class.

Answer Key

1. background	5. to the left
2. next to	6. behind
3. front	7. left
4. right	8. foreground

Language for Writing: Describing Emotions

In describing a photograph, students can say how they think the people in the picture feel or they can report how the image makes them feel. Point out the degrees of formality in the information in the box. Students can talk about themselves (*The image makes me feel . . .*), or they can be more formal and talk about how any viewer might feel.

Exercise B.

- Ask students to work individually to unscramble the sentences to practice writing about feelings and thoughts.

- Check the answers as a class by asking volunteers to write the sentences on the board.

Answer Key

1. The boy seems happy and relaxed.
2. The dead gorilla makes me feel angry and sad.
3. The water looks cool and refreshing.
4. This image reminds people of environmental problems.
5. The young girl makes us think of a famous sculpture.

Exercise C.

- Students work individually to choose a photo from the unit and describe it.

- Ask students to join a partner and take turns reading their sentences aloud and guessing which photo is being described.

Answer Key

Possible answer (for the photo on the top of page 186):
Description: The three laughing women in the foreground are covered with red paint.
How it makes me feel / What it makes me think of: The photo reminds me of happy times playing paintball with my brother.

Writing Skill: Using Supporting Ideas in a Descriptive Paragraph

This skill section describes a useful process for describing images. The steps and components are:

1. a topic sentence that identifies the picture and gives an opinion about it
2. a reason why you like the photo
3. a detail to support that reason
4. another reason why you like it
5. a detail to support reason two
6. a concluding sentence that sums up the paragraph

Sometimes this is called the "sandwich approach" to paragraph writing, where steps 1 and 6 are the "bread" and steps 2 through 5 are the "meat and vegetables." Drawing this image on the board will help visual learners remember the process.

Exercise D. | Describing a Photograph

- Have students work individually or in pairs to identify and label the different parts of a paragraph. Tell them to write the letters in the appropriate boxes.

- Check the answers as a class.

Answer Key

In order of appearance in the paragraph: a, c, e, d, f, b

Writing Task: Drafting
(page 200)

Exercise A. | Brainstorming

- Ask students to work individually to quickly look through the entire book for six photographs they really like.

- Put students into pairs to discuss why they think each of their chosen photos is great.

- Have a few volunteers tell the class why they like the photos they chose.

Exercise B. | Planning

- Go over the steps in this exercise. Model how this works by putting a chart on the board. Remind students that complete sentences are not necessary at this stage, and that it is more important to focus on their ideas than on grammar or spelling.

Best photo	Mother carrying baby in foreground, page 42
Reason 1	Vivid with lots of color
detail	Striped shawl
Reason 2	Moment in time
detail	Baby looking directly at viewer, mother making eye contact with friend
feeling	Happy, baby starting to be individual, aware of world

- Allow time for students to work individually.

TIP Ask the class if they know how to find out who took their favorite photograph. A list of photo credits starts in the front of the book on page xvi and continues on page 224. Names of photographers are listed by the page where the image appears.

Exercise C. | Draft 1

As students write their paragraphs, walk around and offer help if asked. Refrain from any type of error correction at this point.

Writing Task: Revising and Editing *(page 201)*

Exercise D. | Peer Evaluation

- Quickly discuss the three steps in this exercise. Note the emphasis on logical order and on providing examples and details.

- Make sure that both members of the pair have equal time to give feedback.

Exercise E. | Draft 2

- Walk around and monitor students as they work. Provide assistance as needed.

- Remind students to use the feedback they got from their partner.

Exercise F. | Editing Practice

- Go over the information in the box.

- Allow time for students to work individually to edit the eight sentences.

- Check the answers by asking students to read out the correct sentences and explain the errors.

Answer Key

1. Next **to** the boys is a large group of elephants.
2. In this photo, a mother is sitting between her son **and** her daughter.
3. A young girl in a pink coat is standing behind her brother.
4. **In** the middle of the scene, there is a small yellow fish.
5. **In** the foreground, we see a small dog in a green sweater.
6. There is a large tree behind the little boy.
7. There is a baby **on** the right of her mother.
8. The children are beside the water buffaloes.

Writing Task: Editing

(page 202)

Exercise G. | Editing Checklist

- Go over the sentences in the editing checklist.
- Allow time for students to read and edit their work.
- Ask for some examples of each type of error.

Exercise H. | Final Draft

Have students complete their final draft, and then collect their work.

Unit Quiz

- Students can work in groups to answer the questions.
- Encourage students to refer back to the relevant pages of the unit to find the answers.
- To do the quiz as a competition, you can have students work in teams.

Answer Key

1. moment	**5.** language
2. visible	**6.** calm
3. flashbulb memory	**7.** penguin
4. time	**8.** supporting

IDEAS FOR... **Expansion**

As a capstone project, students could organize a photo exhibition called "A Picture Is Worth 1,000 Words" to make the point that a graphic image can convey many complex ideas that the viewer instantly understands. For photographs, have students visit the Photo of the Day section of the National Geographic Photography website http://photography.nationalgeographic.com/photography/photo-of-the-day/?source=NavPhoPOD to explore the range of photographs there. Ask them to select one they really like and print it or download it to a computer. Then students describe the photo using all the skills they have developed in this course. Students can exhibit their photos and writing in the classroom or briefly present them to the rest of the class.

Life in a Day

Complete the outline as you read *A Day on Planet Earth*.

| Who did what? | ➡ | Film director _____ and his _____ produced a _____ movie called *Life in a Day*. |

| When? | ➡ | On a single day— _____ — in _____ . |

| How many? | ➡ | People in _____ countries uploaded _____ videos to YouTube—more than _____ hours. |

| What did Macdonald understand? | ➡ | What may be _____ to one person may be _____ to another. |

| Questions the team asked: | ➡ | Some answers they got: |

| What do you _____ most? | ➡ | • _____ and _____
• _____ and _____ cars
• a pet _____ and a _____ |

| What do you _____? | ➡ | • imaginary _____ and real-life _____
• _____ are going to eat their _____
• guns, _____, the loss of _____ |

| Why was the film possible? | ➡ | Because of the way people are all _____ |

Learning Experiences

Complete the diagram as you read *Global Education*.

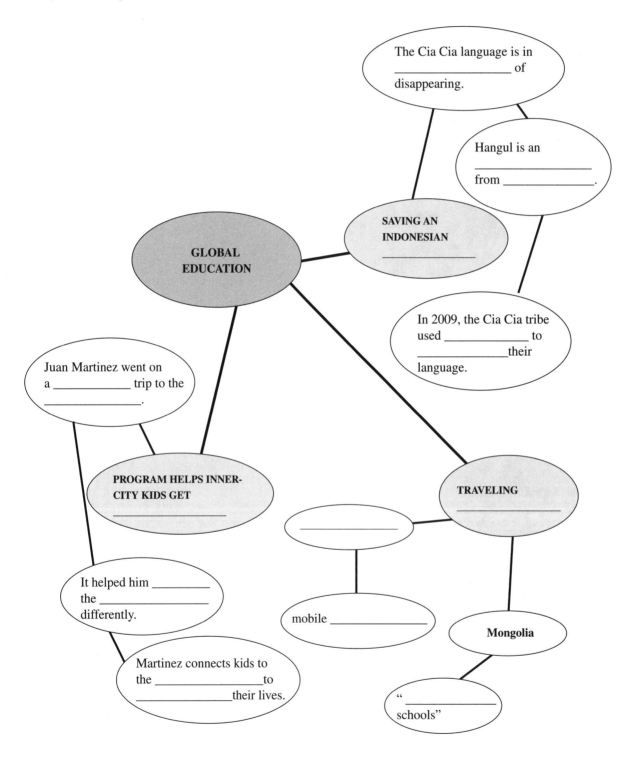

The Cia Cia language is in _____ of disappearing.

Hangul is an _____ from _____.

SAVING AN INDONESIAN _____

In 2009, the Cia Cia tribe used _____ to _____ their language.

GLOBAL EDUCATION

Juan Martinez went on a _____ trip to the _____.

PROGRAM HELPS INNER-CITY KIDS GET _____

It helped him _____ the _____ differently.

Martinez connects kids to the _____ to _____ their lives.

TRAVELING _____

_____

mobile _____

Mongolia

" _____ schools"

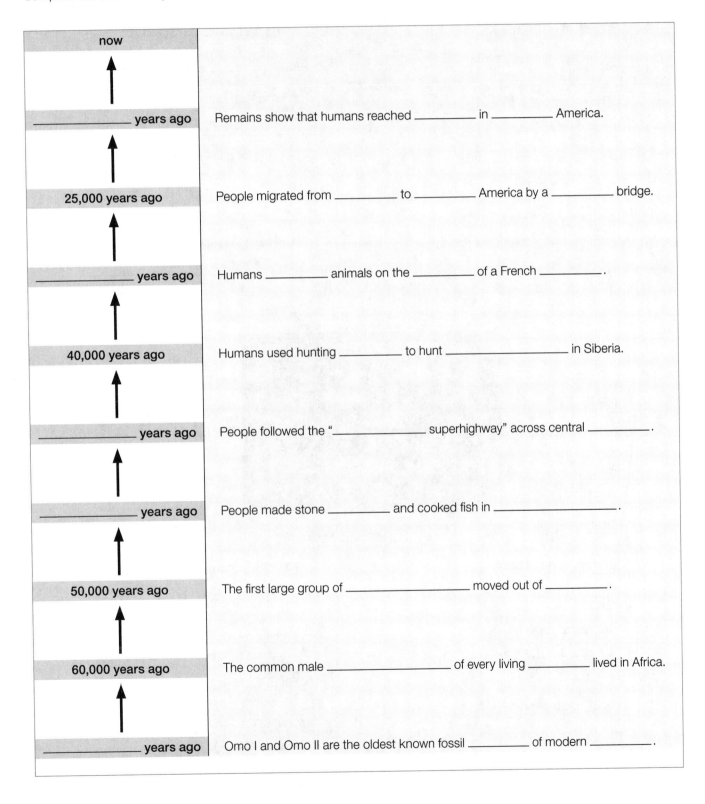

Family Ties

Complete the time line as you read *Our Family Journey*.

now

_____ years ago

Remains show that humans reached _____ in _____ America.

25,000 years ago

People migrated from _____ to _____ America by a _____ bridge.

_____ years ago

Humans _____ animals on the _____ of a French _____ .

40,000 years ago

Humans used hunting _____ to hunt _____ in Siberia.

_____ years ago

People followed the "_____ superhighway" across central _____ .

_____ years ago

People made stone _____ and cooked fish in _____ .

50,000 years ago

The first large group of _____ moved out of _____ .

60,000 years ago

The common male _____ of every living _____ lived in Africa.

_____ years ago

Omo I and Omo II are the oldest known fossil _____ of modern _____ .

The Trouble with Trash

Complete the diagram as you read *Garbage Island*.

❶ What it is

- It's a collection of _____ of bits of _____ and other objects.

- Much of the _____ comes from everyday objects that people _____ _____, such as _____ bags and _____ bottles.

❸ Why it's dangerous

- Sea _____ eat plastic _____ and die.

- _____ may die if they eat plastic _____ that hold six-packs of soda.

- _____ near the ocean surface _____ sunlight from reaching deeper water; lack of _____ kills _____ and _____.

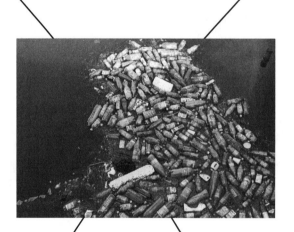

❷ How it got there

- Pacific Ocean _____ bring objects together and cause them to _____ around in a giant _____.

- The _____ movement stops the _____ from _____.

- New objects _____ the spinning _____, and the island _____ bigger.

❹ What people are doing

- An _____ named David de Rothschild is sailing a _____ made of _____ bottles to _____ people about the _____ of ocean _____.

- Environmental engineer _____ _____ is building a _____ that _____ pieces of _____. He hopes to _____ it to _____ _____ garbage in the Pacific.

The World in Our Kitchen

Complete the outline as you read *From Farm to Fork*.

The Environmental Argument

Locally produced foods	➜ consume much less _____ for transport.
	➜ use less _____ and _____ for packaging.
	➜ use fewer oil-based _____ and _____ .

The Carnegie Mellon University Study

➜ What you _____ may be more _____ than where the _____ comes from.

➜ _____ production requires a lot of _____, _____, and _____ .

➜ Cows also produce _____, a _____ gas.

➜ Not eating _____ is probably _____ for the global _____ than eating

only _____ _____ foods.

The Health Argument

Locavores feel that local food is _____ and _____ than food

produced by _____ companies.

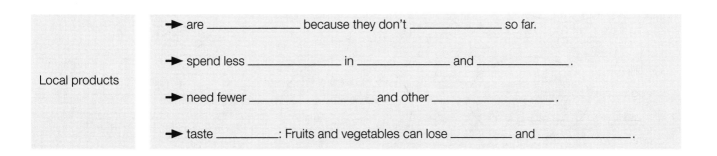

Local products	➜ are _____ because they don't _____ so far.
	➜ spend less _____ in _____ and _____ .
	➜ need fewer _____ and other _____ .
	➜ taste _____: Fruits and vegetables can lose _____ and _____ .

Future Living

Complete the diagram as you read *How Will We Live?*

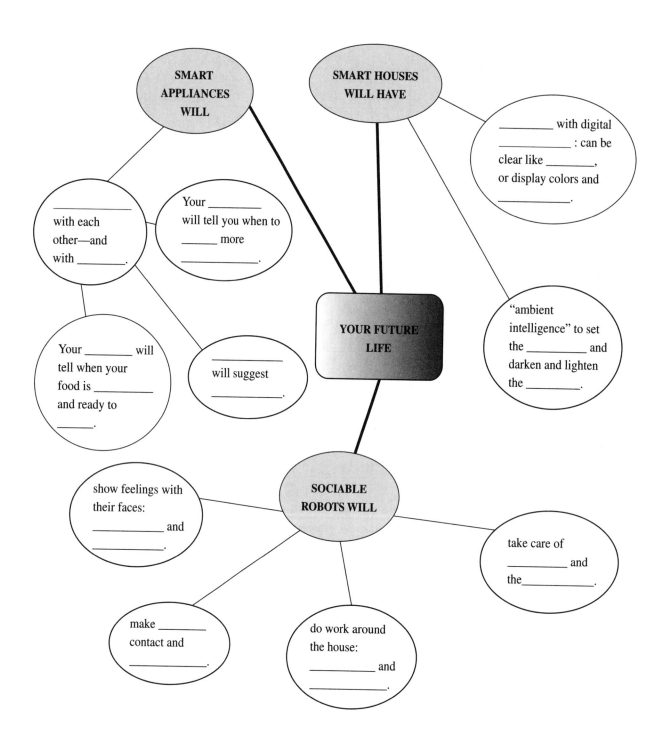

Exploration and Discovery

Complete sentences a–g below as you read *In Stanley's Footsteps*. Then write the letters of the events in the correct order on the map.

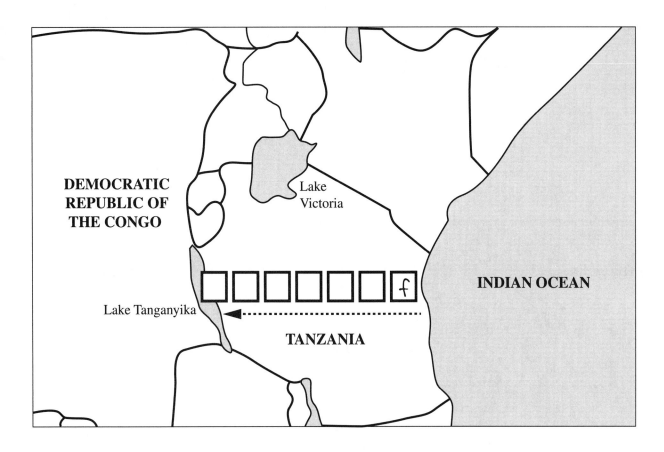

a. It's very hot as they climb the _____ Mountains and then very windy that night.

b. Crowds of people dance and clap to greet them as they arrive in _____.

c. They eat some insect _____, and one team member gets very _____.

d. The team kayaks on a river to a swamp filled with _____ and _____.

e. Now they are in _____ country, and the _____ of dead animals cover the ground.

f. The expedition is about _____ miles from the start and has more than _____ miles to go.

g. It's so _____ in the morning in the misty mountains that the team can't start a _____.

Musicians with a Message

As you read *Music for Change*, complete the Venn diagram to compare Jason Mraz, Zinhle Thabethe, and Arn-Chorn Pond. How are they alike? How are they different?

Jason Mraz

Zinhle Thabethe

Arn Chorn-Pond

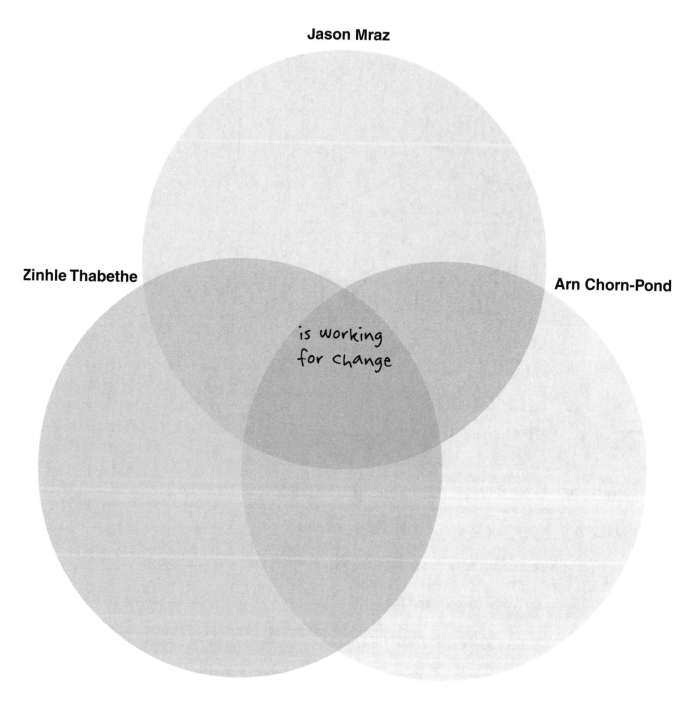

is working
for change

Behavior

Complete the reporter's notes as you read *Meet the Dog Whisperer.*

Cesar Millan: an animal _____ – helps _____ and dog _____
deal with their _____.

He says the biggest mistake people make with dogs: We _____ dogs.

Why people like certain kinds of dogs:

A pit bull represents _____, _____, and _____.

A small poodle is _____ and _____.

Milan's approach to helping dog owners:

- If you don't tell a _____ what to _____, it will _____ you what to _____.

- You don't _____ a dog if it would like to _____ –
  you put on the _____ and _____.

What his parents think about his work:

- They wanted him to become a _____, like a _____ or
  _____.

- They don't understand why people pay him for _____.

What he thinks dogs teach us:

- to _____ in the _____

- _____ (dogs will never _____ to you)

Millan believes _____ behave better than _____.

The Power of Image

Complete the information about the photographs as you read *How Photography Connects Us.*

Photographer	What the photo shows	Why it is a powerful image
Jonas Bendiksen	a Dharavi street coming _____ for a Hindu _____ in Mumbai, India	It shows the _____ and _____ of a _____ in a slum area.
Elmar Rubio	his two _____ throwing their _____ into the strong wind of an approaching _____	It _____ a special _____ in time.
Brent Stirton	villagers carrying a silverback _____ named Senkwekwe, who was illegally _____	The photo creates a _____ narrative to make people aware of the _____ facing wild gorillas.
Brian Skerry	a thresher _____ caught in a _____ net	The picture shows how millions of sharks are _____ each year, mostly for their _____ .
Randy Olson	a _____ Mbuti boy getting ready for a _____ , and a young Mbuti _____	The photo looks something like Degas's bronze _____ of a ballet _____ .